Youth Work in the 1970s

Youth Work in the 1970s

Fred Milson MA BD PHD

Head of Youth and Community Service Section
Westhill College of Education Birmingham

Routledge & Kegan Paul   London

First published 1970
by Routledge & Kegan Paul Ltd
Broadway House, 68–74 Carter Lane,
London, E.C.4
Printed in Great Britain by
Clarke, Doble & Brendon Ltd,
Plymouth
© Fred Milson 1970
ISBN 07100 6865 4

Contents

To Catherine Margaret Milson

Introduction

The division of human history into decades is, of course, an entirely artificial arrangement made for the convenience of historians, public speakers and politicians.

Yet 1 January 1970 was an important date in the history of this country and particularly for the young: it marked the time when 18 became the legal age of majority. Young people are now able to do a number of things, such as getting married or taking out a mortgage, for which previously they had to seek their parents' approval.

In a lesser way too, the date was important for the youth of Britain for it marked the time from which it was hoped the new policy for Youth Service (outlined in the report 'Youth and Community Work in the 70s') would begin to be implemented. The Albemarle Report planned for the 60s. It was on 26 March 1967 in the House of Commons, that Mr Denis Howell, M.P., announced the setting-up of two committees to undertake a complete review of the Service— one for the younger adolescents and the other for the older.[1] The report of these two committees has now been issued and there is currently a discussion throughout educational and social work circles on its relevance and feasibility.

Perhaps no author has a right to include an apologia. But this work has a conscious purpose and it is written from an acknowledged point of view. Possible misunderstanding may be avoided if I make clear what those two factors are.

First, then, a word about the constituency. It is hoped that what is written here will have some value for the full-time youth worker, but the present volume has a wider audience in mind; it includes 'spare-time' workers, leaders, helpers, uniformed organization officials, members of management committees, councillors, parents—and all those who have an interest in the social education of young people. That is why, throughout, wherever possible, it seeks to avoid technical language.

INTRODUCTION

I have become convinced that in Youth Service, a gulf has opened up between many of the theoreticians and many of the practitioners. (This conviction has been re-inforced during the last few years when as chairman of one of the above committees, I have visited many parts of the country and talked with the shop-floor operatives of Youth Service.) The latter have been puzzled by the technical language of the former; some of them have been a little disturbed by questions about their motives. Perfectionist demands lead to disappointment and a feeling of futility. Many of the books which have been written on this and related subjects have been too difficult for some of the part-time operators to understand; and a few of the professionals too. There has been a tendency to over-intellectualize the whole subject. A few extreme theoreticians have even appeared half to suggest that we should suspend all operations until research findings have established the exact situation. (As Howard Jones has pointed out, the same procedure for juvenile delinquency would be disastrous.[2]) That seems to me to exhibit a touching faith in the reliability, stability and usefulness of research findings.

I have no wish to be misunderstood. Youth workers need to raise their skills; they need to examine and refine their motives; youth work is a subject deserving of study; reliable research findings are necessary for a more efficient service. But the theoreticians ought at least to have remembered the counsel which is often given to the apprentice social educators of the young—'Start with them where they are'. (And there is nothing patronizing about this advice since if the 'spare-timers' had to explain the expertise of their jobs to the theoreticians, they also would have to labour at the problems of communication.)

The present volume tries to avoid this error. That is one of the reasons why there are so few footnotes and further references. 'Youth Leadership' is essentially a human process and there are shorter and better-known words for most of the jargon that has become fashionable.

Again, this is not primarily a plea for the spending of more public money on the Service, though that is desirable and would I think be forthcoming, if the urgency and the promise of social education were more widely appreciated.

Nor does it seek to be a 'how to do it' book full of practical suggestions for the revival of flagging groups; for though scattered throughout are specific hints for improvement, it is more concerned with ideas about the Service.

Finally it is not a history of Youth Service, though there is some history in it, and I would agree that we are unlikely to progress unless we give some attention to 'the pit from which we were dug'.

What is written here is often one man's view. Admittedly—on the basis of experience—I have come to certain conclusions, which I am glad to expose to criticism. If that is called 'subjective', I do not object for I cannot understand how else a man may write.

From my standpoint then, I see a new emphasis in thinking about youth work in the last ten years—a development that was healthy, necessary, chastening. It criticized the unconscious paternalistic assumptions of many of the old ways of working; it called for a more professional approach and asked for leaders who would be self-aware, objective, who knew that they might be satisfying their own needs rather than the needs of young people; it encouraged a leadership that was skilful in group work and casework and was not merely providing facilities, and a leadership, moreover, that was prepared to examine the work in the light of the total social situation.

As I say, these developments were good and raised the standards on the whole. But in some cases we have been so anxious to embrace the new that we have carelessly thrown the old away, not noticing its well-tried value. We ought of course to have sought to combine the best of the old with the best of the new. Perhaps in this we have been too much influenced by the spirit of the age; we have been told so often that this is a time of rapid change that any preference for the old promotes feelings of guilt.

Youth Service has had to operate during the last ten years at a time when people have been saying things like 'the pace of change is such that no person over 35 can hope to understand what is happening to a teenager'. This has been reinforced by some of the writers on youth work who have depicted adults as ogres seeking to deny to the young the emancipation on which they are hell-bent. Perhaps some of those writers are projecting into the situation their own adolescent struggles for freedom. Of course there is some truth in this interpretation, but I think it has been much overdone: the research findings of the Eppels and Musgrove show that it is still common for many adolescents to be looking to their parents for support and approval. Even to hint that wisdom began with the present generation of teenagers is unfair to them as well as being ludicrous. The abdication of adults from all positions of responsibility in relation to the young is at least as bad as paternalism. In twenty years' time, it may well be that many of the present teenagers will be saying to their elderly parents, 'But why didn't you tell us? And make us see? You had the experience.'

Equally with the gold of the new developments has come the dross of a neglect of the emotional factors in leadership, again perhaps by writers who were a little fearful of the emotional forces in their own lives. To caricature the situation, it almost seems at times as though the desire is to replace the warm, human, caring person with the cold, detached person who has a correct set of techniques. Books that have written openly of moral and spiritual motivations and ideals, like Reg Keeble's *A Life full of Meaning*,[3] have been sneered at in professional circles.

We ought to be reminded, I think, that the youth worker is an artist rather than a scientist, needing inspiration more than definitions. Enthusiasm is not to be lightly dismissed; nor is that faith in people's possibilities which keeps many a fallible leader going through defeat and discouragement.

I have been involved in many discussions about youth work in the past few years. A few of them I have found arid and too theoretical. At such times, I have wished to have a young man and a young woman present, or, at least, a picture of them, to be able to say at a fruitless point in the discussion, 'This is what we are talking about.'

With all our increased knowledge of psychology and sociology, and with our improved techniques, I cannot help wondering how much better we understand at the finger-tip point of contact with the adolescents of Britain. The words and the experience of the adolescent Gavin Maxwell are salutary for all concerned with Youth Service.

My final shame was still to come. Quite early on in the meal my knife slipped on the plate and a large green pea shot into the middle of the table, leaving an irregular spoor of gravy behind it. There it lay, seeming to me as big as a football while course succeeded course and the footman ignored it with studious spite. It was still there when they cleared everything else away and brought the dessert plates; it was still there when the ladies left the room and I was able to move a few places up the table and disown it for ever. . . . Among all the works on adolescent psychology that I have read I have not found one whose author seems to remember what it is like to be an adolescent. They state academic truths, but the standpoint is external, as detached as if they were recording experimental data on the behaviour of laboratory rats, and no one can remember what it feels like to be a laboratory rat. . . .

The abyss that gapes between the average adult and the average adolescent is not fundamentally a failure of knowledge—though that too exists in the great majority of cases—but a failure of understanding that is less excusable, for it is due to a wilful, often compulsive forgetfulness.[4]

Notes:

1   Hansard. 26 March 1967.
2   'For if we wait until all is known, we may wait too long.' Howard Jones, *Crime in a changing society*, Pelican, p. 163.
3   Published by Pergamon Press.
4   Gavin Maxwell, *The House of Elrig*, Longmans 1965, Pan Books 1968, pp. 168–9.

1

The long history of Youth Service

People often talk as though Youth Service has only a short history. They see it as beginning in this country with the issue of circular 1486 in November 1939. Or they may even think of it as an invention of Lady Albemarle and the members of her committee who issued their report in 1960. Both these events are important landmarks; the first saw the entry of the government into leisure-time provision for adolescents and the beginning of a partnership between statutory and voluntary agencies; the second injected new life into what was fairly described as a dying service.

But neither of those events marked the beginnings of Youth Service; indeed, as we hope to show very soon, the beginnings of Youth Service are lost in the mists of antiquity and it is almost as old as human society itself.

However, even if we confine our attention to 'organized youth work' and to Britain alone, the history of the Service is longer than is commonly imagined. Any other picture is grossly unfair to the voluntary organizations which began to care at least 150 years before the State took a hand in the leisure-time social education of adolescents.

It is easy to judge the educationists and social workers of another age from the vantage point of the twentieth century and find their methods and motives unsatisfactory; but clearly we should employ historical perspective and see them against the background of the standards and practices of their own times.

Hannah More began her schools and clubs towards the end of the eighteenth century meeting opposition to her educational plans for young people from farmers who complained, 'We shan't have a boy to plough or a wench to dress a shoulder of mutton.' It was in 1780 that Robert Raikes, the proprietor of the *Gloucester Journal*, opened his first Sunday Schools, motivated, it is said, partly by the

1

disturbances which interrupted his own peaceful Sabbath and were caused by the youngsters of the district who were not at work in the local pin factory on one day of the week.

In the nineteenth century, Neumann, one of the unsung heroes of the boys' clubs movement, found 150 homeless boys in London, and one who slept inside the roller in Regent's Park every night, his emaciated body being thin enough to go through the railings.

The nineteenth century saw the foundation in this country of the Y.M.C.A., the Y.W.C.A., the Girls' Friendly Society, the Boys' Brigade, the Working Boys' Clubs and the Working Girls' Clubs: the twentieth century brought the Girls' Life Brigade, the Boy Scouts, the Cubs, the Girl Guides, the Brownies, the N.A.B.C., the N.A.Y.C. and the National Federation of Young Farmers Clubs (formed by the Ministry of Agriculture)—all before November 1939. Many of these movements spread overseas. Today, the Boys' Brigade captain and the club leader and many more, struggling to do their best to facilitate a 'fuller life' for young people, struggling against difficulties and facing the challenge of new standards—they are part of a long and not ignoble tradition.

But it is our intention to suggest a far wider interpretation of the term 'Youth Service' than the common meaning of organized youth movements and hence to indicate an even longer history.

Adolescence is a universal phenomenon though its duration, content and meaning varies widely from one society to another. But generally one can say that it is a human experience at the meeting place of many changes—physical, physiological, emotional—and also, social. It is not merely that the adolescent has a new body with a new set of desires; he also has a new status in society and is expected to behave in the appropriate way. 'Act your age,' we may say to him. It is the recognition of the role-change in adolescence which gives 'Youth Service' its universal character. For most societies have realized that there are not two stages in the individual's life—childhood and adulthood—but at least three, the third being adolescence when he may have stopped being a child but not yet become completely an adult. And most societies have made some arrangements to help the individual to achieve this change, no doubt almost invariably for the sake of the community as well as the individual. This is what we are choosing to call in this widest possible interpretation 'Youth Service'. Moreover, there have usually been in societies those who had the special responsibility for helping with this role-change, making the arrangements and organizing the ceremonies, say: and these we choose to identify as 'youth workers'.

In the Bible, there is an appealing story of profound psychological insight in I Samuel III vv. 1–10. A young boy called Samuel, who has been dedicated to the service of the Temple by his parents, hears a voice calling his name in the night. He is sure that this is the voice of his old master, Eli; and three times he goes to Eli, only to be assured that the call did not come from him. In the end, the old man has the sense to see what is happening and tells the boy that if he hears the voice again he has to say, 'Speak; for thy servant heareth'. For he realizes that it is the voice of God, or in psychological language, the voice of his awakening nature. That is 'Youth Service' and Eli was a youth worker, though he does not appear to have been conspicuously successful with his own sons; he interpreted Samuel's present experience for him and pointed the way to the future.

Here is the story of two individuals, but one of the most rewarding questions to ask about any society, ancient or modern, is, 'How do they help the young people to become adults?' And some of the most fascinating and colourful material in anthropological writings is in answer to that question as the readers of Margaret Mead and Ruth Benedict[1] know well.

It is common knowledge today that in earlier societies, smaller and usually agrarian societies, there were the initiation rites which marked clearly the passage of the youngster to adult status. They provided a public spectacle saying to the whole community, 'He is a man now: treat him as such'; and they provided a private experience saying to the individual, 'You are a man now; behave as such.' Of course, they usually included a form of examination, testing the youngster's knowledge of community laws, his acquisition of community skills and in some cases his ability to bear pain. Clearly the ceremonies would take place only in a community where the behaviour of the individual was laid down by the community as a whole, where there were accepted traditions and strong social control. 'Youth Service' may be said to be institutionalized in these kinds of society; it is based on traditional beliefs and ceremonies which apply to everybody.

Some of those practices survive but significantly they exist in what are called 'primitive' societies, that is, modern societies which usually through isolation have not been affected by twentieth century ways of thinking and living together. A few years ago, a television programme showed the 'tree-diving' exploits of the male adolescents of a South Seas Island. Each youngster jumped from a tall tree, with ropes attached to his legs to land in a bed of rushes. The myth was that they were commemorating the brave deed of one of their ancestors who thus escaped from an enemy more heavily-armed than he. But as each youngster accomplished this hazardous feat, a woman in the crowd—his mother in fact—threw away a male doll, thereby symbolizing that her boy had become a man. Michael Banton[2] tells of the Poro in parts of modern Sierra Leone and Liberia; they are the 'youth workers' of the country. In a series of pantomimic activities, they raid the villages and take away all the boys who are ready for initiation and carry them into the forest. Here they are circumcised and given special training, taught a number of crafts and undergo some rigorous hardships. 'The most important factor in the bush training, however, is the psychological experience, which makes the initiates feel themselves confident adults, knowing the secrets of men and exercising control over village affairs.'[3] When they are brought back to the village in some districts there is an elaborate pretence that they have never been there before. They are shown where to fetch water, where the different families live, and given the names of old friends as though they are meeting them for the first time: they are given new names and anybody using their old name can be fined by the Poro: all this symbolizing that they are new people with a new status.

Of course, it is all very different in a modern industrial society and the difference today is commonly expressed by saying that the position of the adolescent is not defined by the society and the role-change to adulthood is not clearly marked by a set of ceremonies which everybody has to undergo. What has happened? Societies have become larger and more complex: there are fewer common beliefs and accepted traditions: fewer people are born and live and die in the same neighbourhood; fewer people remain in that station of life in which they were born; change discredits the past.

It is in this situation that 'Youth Service' as the term is generally understood—that is, in the sense of organized youth movements—springs up. When the society as a whole can no longer undertake the social education of all its young, youth movements attempt to fill the gap. As Eisenstadt has pointed out, youth movements do not develop in those societies where the family can adequately prepare the youngster for life as an adult in the community, where, for example, the boy learns his trade from his father and the family work together.[4]

The growth of industrialization is the main factor which lies behind the new situation. Prior to the Industrial Revolution in Britain there was a settled society where 'the boys helped on the farm, hunted and fished; the girls helped in the dairy, learned to cook and preserve and the use of samples, even the toddlers scared the birds. Then young people had a well-defined, if not always, enviable place in society, and the status accorded to the place.'[5] With the Industrial Revolution, natural communities were broken down; thousands of workers lived close to factories in houses huddled together; and the young were often given dull and dangerous work; and the position of the young in society became undefined.

In this social milieu there appeared the voluntary youth organization; no doubt the pioneers and early workers were driven by a variety of motives; and some of them not so worthy, like fear of the threat to their own privileged position; but what is equally clear is that better motives were present from the beginning.

It is the presence of these constant factors in the emergence of youth work which may account for the fact that wherever it occurs in any strength, matters of social conscience—and, therefore, very often of religious conviction—a concern for education, a political awareness of the significance of youth in society, and an absorbing interest in adolescents, as political leaders, as potential citizens or delinquents—form some of the main motivating forces of those organizing or sponsoring such groups.[6]

To this discussion, we return later.

THE AGE OF VOLUNTARYISM

There is a pattern of social and education work in Britain which is often repeated. The first to see the need are private men and women who organize to meet it; they do not wait for laws or public funds, which in any case might not be forthcoming. But soon the pioneering efforts of the voluntaryists have called public attention to the need and the government begins to attempt the work. An additional reason is that by this time the voluntary organizations have been found to lack the resources in money and man power to meet the total need. A final stage is reached when statutory and voluntary agencies join forces in a partnership. This, briefly, is the path which has been taken by organized Youth Service in this country. This section is concerned to take a quick look at the 150 years of voluntaryism and see how it led to State participation and partnership.

Judgments on this long period of voluntaryism vary wildly; there are those who point the finger of scorn at its deficiencies; by contrast are those who settle on the virtues of voluntaryism, treat it as a Golden Age and long nostalgically for its return. Perhaps, as in many other arguments, a balanced point of view sees both good and bad in these pioneering efforts. We shall suggest that whilst we must not be lacking in praise, yet there is a serious danger if we allow these earlier forms of Youth Service to influence too much our philosophy and practice in the present. The compassion of yesterday becomes the oppression of today if the earlier forms are slavishly copied. It is perilously easy to assume that the patterns of youth work which have been inherited in our generation are inevitable.

Some of the critics of the age of voluntaryism simply lack historical perspective; they are judging nineteenth century people by twentieth century standards; they expect moral miracles in the sense that they criticize pioneers for not consistently acting against the spirit of their age. It is not enough apparently that they showed a sensitivity that was unusual at the time; they are condemned for not being perfect. For example, Davies and Gibson comment on the pioneers, 'Without doubt they were altruistic; they opposed other possible types of provision and offered their own because with deep sincerity they believed they were far the best thing for the young. But the motivations of many of them cannot have been so simple or unmixed.'[7] In other words, they were human beings.

In particular, they have been criticized for devoting a large part of their effort to Christian evangelism, teaching the young to read the Bible (which was also often teaching them to read for the first time) and devoting time to prayer. Whilst there would be a general dislike of indoctrination today, the strength of this criticism obviously depends on the critic's own feelings about the Christian faith, its truth and relevance. But at the time, before the development in educational theory had stressed the freedom and personal growth of the pupil, it is hard to see how this approach was anything but inevitable. They have been criticized also for knowing what was good for young people and not allowing youngsters to work things out for themselves —when 'spontaneous youth groups' are only a slow twentieth century development. In no age can youth workers be expected to effect a complete social revolution which answers the objection that they could have encouraged commercial provision—at a time when commercial entertainment was suspect as being harmful—or persuaded the government to take a more active part—at a time when laissez-faire notions were powerful, suggesting that good government interferes as little as possible in the lives of the people. A more balanced view is given by Macalister Brew: 'It is true that much of the work was often tinged with patronage and flavoured with a kind of piety which is distasteful today, but that it made an incalculable contribution to the lives of many young people in an age when few cared for them is indisputable and should not lightly be dismissed.'[8] Nor is the charge that those early worker enthusiasts were always social workers—and never social reformers—that in fact they cared for the victims of an evil system without ever seeking to change the system—to be made lightly or without qualification. Some of them agitated for the raising of the school-leaving age and their efforts were also related to legislation such as the Children and Young Persons Act 1918.

On the other hand, the fulsome praise of the volunteers needs abating. Such assessors often overlook the part played by unconscious motives in the work of the pioneers and they are tempted to judge every worker in the movement by the statements of aims put forward by highly articulate founding fathers like Baden-Powell and William Smith. Moreover, voluntary organizations suffer the fate of many institutions. They spring up spontaneously in answer to a need and flourish by a ready response; but when the first fine careless days are over, they pass to a defensive stage of self-preservation. The movement begins to be, not only a means of service, but a focal point of vested interests. One sees the traditional voluntary organization struggling to adjust to the times, whilst retaining its recognisable historical identity. Whilst it is true that the voluntary organizations are more flexible than the statutory agency and can promote new forms of service, because of their traditions they may find it more difficult to adjust to the spirit of the age. Sometimes the new wine demands new bottles. There are three areas in which this can be observed among voluntary youth movements. First, they segregated the sexes in their history and there has been a struggle in this country to have mixed youth work accepted. Second, they began by being committed to self-conscious purpose—learning to read, to acquire a skill or a pattern of accepted behaviour—and they have had to adjust to a situation where just 'having fun' is seen to be a worthy objective. Thirdly, they

7

began with a religious commitment and they have had to adjust to a situation where having faith is less a condition of social acceptance and more of an individual option.

It was in the twentieth century that the conclusion was forced upon those who were concerned with the young that good as the work of the voluntary organizations might be, it could not cater for all the nation's youth who needed the Service. It was not always wide enough since if it was the only provider, it sometimes offered a service with strings attached. A scout troop or a church club in a village may do excellent work, but if either are the only form of youth work available a youngster may not be able to have his fun without committing himself to an ideology. Moreover, the resources were not forthcoming. Increased taxation after the First World War dealt a heavy blow at voluntary work. The situation was helped by the generosity during the 30s of the Carnegie Trust and the King George's Jubilee Trust Fund, but there was still not enough in the kitty for a national service.

A number of reports produced in the 1930s showed twin facts which pointed in the direction of voluntary organizations being partners but not sole providers, since in any case the days of laissez-faire were over and the government was playing an increasing part in the daily lives of the citizens. The first discovery was that the voluntary organizations were not meeting the total need. In September 1939, there were about 4 million young people between 14 and 20 in the United Kingdom; only half a million were associated with voluntary organizations. The second discovery, from a number of sources, was that the economic depression of the 1920s and 1930s had been a tragic time for the young people of this country.[9] The British Medical Association issued a report in 1936 which painted a gloomy picture of the state of health of the nation's youth and to make matters worse, contrasted the picture with what could be seen in other countries such as Norway, Germany and Czechoslovakia.

Before the issue of circular 1486, there were several attempts, largely abortive, at state participation in the social education of adolescents during their leisure-time. As far back as 1916, as a response to public concern over the rise in juvenile delinquency, the Home Office and the Board of Education combined to set up the Juvenile Organization Committee, a central body with local counterparts. But they withered through lack of support. The Physical Training and Recreation Act of 1937 extended the powers of local authorities to provide recreational facilities and made grants available from the Board of Education and a National Advisory Council; but the war overtook the working out of these measures.

The era of partnership was inaugurated by the issue of circular 1486 by the Board of Education, which authorized grants to support voluntary organizations, made possible the appointment of youth officers and set up local committees with representatives of statutory and voluntary parties.

The age of voluntaryism was over, though it was hoped the voluntary organizations would flourish in a new partnership. They had served well on the whole, but in the nature of the case could not undertake the Youth Service that was demanded. Behind the new arrangements lay social responsibility and anxiety and fears that were sharpened both by alarming reports about the nation's youth, their health and literacy, and by the disruption that everybody knew was coming in war-time conditions.

THE GROWTH OF PARTNERSHIP

The history of war-time Youth Service in this country has been written several times,[10] and we may content ourselves with a brief overall view. There are in fact two separate but related areas to be examined; one, the various policy statements, official and semi-official, which were issued about the Service as a whole and also specifically about training; and the other, the practical developments of the new partnership in the field of Youth work.

Whilst Circular 1486 announced the fact of the partnership and described the broad outlines, it was considered necessary to follow this soon afterwards by Circular 1516 ('The Challenge of Youth') which gave more details of the ways in which the partnership should work. After pointing the moral about the need, in the interests of youth, for combined operations, warning that no single approach was sufficient and pleading for a variety of methods, it argued that there was a common purpose in the many forms—social facilities, physical recreation and continuing education. But perhaps the chief importance of circular 1516 is its explicitness about the work of the newly-formed youth committees. They were to be responsible for an ordered policy, for considering carefully the total needs of young people and for a new initiative which would involve young people in finding 'constructive outlets for their leisure hours and for their voluntary National Service'. 'It is not the task of the local youth committees directly to conduct youth activities, but to strengthen the hands of local authorities and voluntary organizations.'

As the work developed, two questions began to claim attention. What was the purpose of the work? And this question arose because of a general misgiving that clubs were 'only for fun'. How did the Youth Service relate to the rest of the educational system? These themes are the pre-occupation of the two reports issued by the Youth Advisory Council.[11] In view of later developments, an important paragraph in the second report is, 'Whilst we recognize, and indeed assert, that the Youth Service is a part of the educational service of this country, we cannot help feeling that it has been and still is pre-occupied with filling the gaps left by an inadequate national system of full-time education. Inevitably this has tended to introduce a therapeutic element into the content and the techniques of the Youth Service.' Oddly enough in view of this judgment, the report went on to offer as a purpose the promotion and provision of opportunities for participation in activities, 'which are carried on in a community different in its nature from school or work'.

The idea of the integration of Youth Service with other forms of provision, notably educational, keeps appearing in the history of the subject. We ourselves shall have much to say about it later in suggesting plans for a Service more widely-based in the community. There is much to be said for integration, but it can represent for Youth Service possible loss as well as possible gain; the danger is not merely that it loses a separate identity—which could conceivably be a good thing—but that the special contribution to the social education of young people, its outlook and methods, can easily be forgotten. Thus, it is tempting to rescue Youth Service from the no-man's-land by seeing it as part of Further Education and this may work excellently if the officers concerned have an enthusiasm for youth work. In some areas the Youth Service and the Youth Employment Service are joined and this again may serve if the leisure time provision is not neglected under pressures from what will appear more urgent affairs; after all, most people given a choice, will think it more important to fit the youngster to the right job, rather than to the right youth organization.

The issue of integration relates to the last two documents to be mentioned.[12] A government White Paper issued in 1943 suggested a national system of part-time education for all young people between 14 and 18 in county colleges. Youth workers in voluntary organizations were alarmed since they thought their work would suffer; they need not have worried since nothing specific developed from the suggestion. Curiously enough, the Education Act of 1944 did not specifically mention Youth Service, but in a way its provisions are implied in Sections 41 and 52, though since that time it has come under the heading of Further Education. Writing of 1945, Winifred Evans comments, 'At this time, the youth service resembled the position of non-provided Schools at the time of the Education Act of 1902. . . . The relationship between the voluntary youth organizations and the Education Authorities, both central and local, has developed in a similar way, except that the several phases of the process have been compressed, up to this time, into six war years, instead of developing over thirty years of peace.'[13]

During the period under review, there were also a number of reports about the training of full-time leaders. Whilst they revealed a complexity in the subject which continues with us to this day, they also sought to give the full-time youth leader a recognized place in the educational system, with a relevant training and an assured future. The McNair Report[14]—the first official report devoted to the subject—stressed the need for professionals, thought they should be drawn from a wide field and usually be older than teachers when they begin this work, and needed a training which included opportunities for personal development and practical work. Several Universities ran courses of training though all except Swansea had ceased by 1953–4. There was still dissatisfaction about opportunities and it was felt that McNair had not been implemented. Two committees and their reports followed. One sought to link full-time youth leadership with the teaching profession.[15] The other, by way of deliberate reaction, suggested that the profession should include a large number over 25 who had experience of earning their living in industry or commerce or one of the professions.[16]

From the early 1950s to the end of the decade relatively few full-time youth leaders were trained in this country.

Finally, how did the new partnership work out in practice? In a later section we attempt to deal with the deeper issues underlying the new association: here we confine ourselves to a largely factual account.

There were difficulties due to the suspicions of voluntary organizations, both justified and groundless. Some local authorities revealed an abysmal ignorance of the work and intentions of voluntary agencies in their area. But the first response on the whole was good. Local Youth Committees were set up in many places and new enterprises began. Generally speaking, the voluntary organizations extended their work and new civic centres were opened. The 'open' youth club with its staple diet of dancing, listening to modern music, darts and table tennis, became very popular.

War-time conditions not only created difficulties for the work—withdrawing leaders for armed services for example—but in other ways provided opportunities. There was a sense of national solidarity and many youth groups earned prestige by relating their work to war effort. Young people were not afraid to move around in the blackout, especially in the quiet early days of the war, and with many avenues of entertainment closed to them, they crowded into clubs.

Public support helped the work, not only in grants for leaders' salaries and equipment and towards the headquarters expenses of national organizations, but, in for example, the modest rations allowed by the Ministry of Food to youth clubs; the 'canteen' was an important feature of war-time Youth Service. Clubs and organizations flourished and grew and contributed to the morale of young people.

The partnership, though not without failures, succeeded and produced results. (It was not so urgent of course when Britain was fighting to survive to ask teasing questions about the purpose of the work.) So L. J. Barnes could write in 1948, 'The old distinction between official and voluntary agencies is breaking down, as far as youth work is concerned.'[17]

YEARS OF NEGLECT, DISCOURAGEMENT AND DECLINE

It seems a far cry from these exciting days of a new partnership to the Youth Service as the Albemarle Committee found it. For there can be little doubt that Albemarle was a rescue operation; it found the Service in a depressed condition. 'Indeed, it has more than once been suggested to us that the appointment of our own Committee was either "a piece of whitewashing" or an attempt to find grounds for "killing" the service.'[18] In such an atmosphere, morale was low. 'But in general we believe it true to say that those who work in the Service feel themselves neglected and held in small regard, both in educational circles and by public opinion generally. . . . No Service can do its best work in such an atmosphere.'[19] The Report quickly uses words like 'critical', 'urgent' and 'blood-transfusion'.

What went wrong? The root trouble was the withdrawal of financial resources from the Service due to the necessary economies after the war. There were many demands upon the diminished wealth of the country and it could plausibly be argued that some should take precedence over the claims for the support of youth organizations. The housing shortage was acute; many schools had been damaged or destroyed; developments from the 1944 Act called for a vast expenditure: in a few years, the rising birth rate demanded many new schools. Building for youth welfare was stopped. The National Voluntary Youth Organizations were asked to accept a 10 per cent cut in their grants.

They were discouraging days and many professional youth workers left for more hopeful and secure appointments. The promised statement on a national policy was not forthcoming. Youth Service at this time lost public appeal and support for a number of reasons. Many saw it as a war-time measure; others wondered what place it could have if the school-leaving age was to be raised to 16 and county colleges were to be set up.

However, it would be a mistake to think of the years between 1945 and 1960 as entirely barren. A number of surveys and assessments were attempted which have had lasting value; together they make the period a time of creative thinking in the history of the Service. In addition a number of new approaches were advocated though not all of them would receive general acclaim.

L. J. Barnes's two valuable reports came in this period. The first[20] gave an encouraging account of what was being accomplished in an English county: the second[21] praised the partnership that existed and pleaded for more co-ordination of effort, research and experiment. King George's Jubilee Trust also sponsored a conference at Ashridge: the report[22] issued in 1951, stressed the value of present partnership and asked for more, pointed to the urgent need for training schemes for leaders, full-time and part-time and rooted youth work unambiguously in the striving for a Christian civilization.[23]

There were, as we have said, several new approaches to developing needs, experimental attempts to serve young people in the commuity. Three organizations were prominent in organizing courses to help with the transition from school to work.[24] Among some there was an emphasis upon outdoor physical adventures, such as mountaineering, as an enjoyable enterprise and a challenge to personal development. It was about this time that club visits overseas began to be organized;

13

there was a stress on self-government by youngsters expressed in the setting up of Members' councils: an increasing number of residential centres made possible short courses of training for leaders.

Despite these new ideas and new practices, the Service as a whole continued to be in a depressed state, chiefly owing to the lack of funds. Very few full-time leaders were being trained mainly because local authorities were reluctant to give grants towards the cost. There were of course other contributing factors such as the withdrawal of boys at 18 by National Service.

The new beginning, when it came, was made possible not only by the arguments from those reports and experiments; and not only by the pressure from educationists, social workers and sociologists who could see the dangers threatening and the opportunities wasted; but not least from a public disquiet which was not uninfluenced by concern about juvenile delinquency and the new teenage 'affluence and independence'.

The public pressure grew: all three political parties promised support; the Minister of Education was accused of apathy and strongly refuted the accusation; a House of Lords' debate was held on the subject. At this time, the Albemarle Committee was appointed—

> To review the contribution which the youth service of England
> and Wales can make in assisting young people to play their part
> in the life of the community, in the light of the changing social
> and industrial conditions, and of current trends in other
> branches of the Education Service, and to advise according
> to what priorities best value can be obtained for the money spent.

WHAT ALBEMARLE PROPOSED

The Albemarle Report cannot be said to have guided Youth Service into new channels, though it certainly provided useful new ideas, in one or two directions. But on the whole it was to be much the same mixture as before with richer ingredients: the Report asked mainly that we should do better what was already being done. For example, it concentrates almost entirely on the expansion of Youth Service within youth organizations, and fails to see the possibility of the growth of youth work in many other settings in the community. However, it succeeded in its main purpose of injecting new life into the ailing Service.

Much of the report is philosophical describing, say, the purpose of Youth Service as social and pastoral (oddly enough 'educational' was left out in this passage because it seems to have been associated with 'formal educational effort') with the famous trilogy of aims—association, training and challenge. A valuable chapter seeks to estimate the contemporary social scene particularly in its effect upon the young. Leadership is carefully scrutinized. There is a historical section. We are not here however concerned primarily with these philosophical questions: they are dealt with elsewhere in the present work. We concentrate now on the precise recommendations of the Albemarle Report and the action which was taken immediately to implement those recommendations.

There are four divisions.

1 *General recommendations* that arose from the Committee's definition. The Youth Service should be available for all young people between 14 and 20: a ten year development programme should be launched: a Youth Service Development Council should be set up: self-determination of members of youth organizations should be encouraged: research and experiment could alone bring the service up to date.

2 *Finance* In fact the Albemarle Report, like Oliver, called for more, from many partners—central government, local government, voluntary sources and young people themselves. Central grants should encourage pioneering work among the 14 to 20 age-group: denominational allegiances should not disqualify voluntary organizations for grants.

3 *Buildings* 'A generous and imaginative building programme' was vital to an expanded Service. The Architects of Buildings' Branch of the Ministry should be asked for designs: high priority should be given to remedying the defects in the provision of facilities for physical recreation.

4 *Training* An emergency scheme should boost the number of full-time workers from 700 in 1960 to 1300 by 1965: courses should be started in some teacher training colleges since the teaching profession was seen as the long term source of supply of full-time operatives: there should be a recognized system of qualifications and recognized salaries and conditions of service for leaders: the training of part-time workers should be separately examined with a view to improvement and expansion.

The above is the barest outline of the Albemarle recommendations.

What was unusual about the Report was that so many of its recommendations for emergency action were so quickly implemented. It was a nice calculation of the ideal and the possible. Administrative arrangements for an expanded Service were in hand before the Committee had finished its sittings. Grants were increased to National Voluntary Youth Organizations and put on a three year basis: denominational groups were recognized as eligible for grant-aid: the Youth Service Development Council was set up and money made available for work of an experimental nature: the National College at Leicester was opened with 95 students before the end of 1961: the Ministry of Education accepted a separate building programme for youth.

The government of the day in feasible areas responded promptly to the challenge of Albemarle, and if the action of the other partners was less precise, it was partly because the challenges to them were frequently more nebulous, as for example that local authorities and voluntary organizations were to work with even closer co-operation. But there was no lack of interest in and generally enthusiasm for, the proposals and not only within the confines of youth work. The general feeling was that a new chapter in the history of the Service had just commenced.

Notes:

1 c.f. Margaret Mead, *Growing up in New Guinea*, Pelican, 1942, and *Coming of Age in Samoa*, Pelican, 1954.
  Also, Ruth Benedict, *Patterns of Culture*, Routledge & Kegan Paul, 1935.
2 Michael Banton, *Roles*, Tavistock, 1965, pp. 94–5.
3 ibid., p. 95.
4 S. M. Eisenstadt, *From Generation to Generation*, Free Press of Glencoe, 1965.
5 J. M. Brew, *Youth and Youth Groups*, Faber & Faber, 1957, p. 115.
6 ibid., p. 117.
7 *The Social Education of the Adolescent*, University of London Press, 1967, p. 32.
8 *Youth and Youth Groups*, Faber & Faber, 1957, p. 119.
9 c.f. *Disinherited Youth; A Survey 1936–1939*, Carnegie United Kingdom, 1943.
10 c.f. *Youth Work in England*, University of Bristol Institute of Education, Publication No. 6, Ed. by P. H. K. Kuenstler, 1954.

Also W. M. Evans, *Young People in Society*, Blackwell, 1966, ch. 2.

11 *Youth Service after the War*, H.M.S.O., 1943.
The Purpose and the Content of the Youth Service, H.M.S.O., 1945.

12 c.f. also *Citizen of Tomorrow*, King George's Jubilee Trust, 1955.

13 ibid., p. 35.

14 *Teachers and Youth Leaders*, Board of Education, H.M.S.O., 1944.

15 *Report of the Committee on the Recruitment Training and Conditions of Service of Youth Leaders and Community Centre Wardens*, Ministry of Education, 1949.

16 *The Recruitment and Training of Youth Leaders and Community Centre Wardens*, H.M.S.O., 1951.

17 *The Outlook for Youth Work*, King George's Jubilee Trust, 1948.

18 *The Youth Service in England and Wales*, H.M.S.O., 1960 (The 'Albemarle' Report), p. 1.

19 ibid., p. 1.

20 *Youth Service in an English County*, King George's Jubilee Trust, 1945.

21 *The Outlook for Youth Work*, King George's Jubilee Trust, 1948.

22 *Youth Service Tomorrow*, King George's Jubilee Trust, 1951.

23 Other reports during this period include:
Pearl Jephcott, *Some Young People*, Allen & Unwin, 1954.
Citizens of Tomorrow, Published by Odhams Press for King George's Jubilee Trust, 1955.

24 They were: Y.M.C.A.: N.A.B.C.: and N.A.G. & M.C. (now N.A.Y.C.).

2

A brief digression—Why is 'Youth Service' constantly under review?

An observer, noticing the constant assessments of the Service, might be forgiven for wondering why this is so and also, when a settled policy is to be adopted and worked. As we have seen, the record is studded with enquiries: numerous pamphlets have dealt with the subject, 'The Purpose of Youth Service' and from 1939 this has been the constant theme of conferences both large and small. The frequent re-assessment in some ways is a source of weakness, sapping the self-confidence and security of those engaged in the work: in other ways, it can be a source of strength since it helps to save youth work from being out of date. But weakness or strength, it is inevitable since there are factors, within society as a whole, and within Youth Service itself, which produce these stocktaking sessions.

As to the first, we have to recognize that most societies are deeply interested in their young people. No doubt some of this interest is humane and springs from a concern to ensure that individual young people 'get the most out of life'. But part of the motivation is functional and springs from the society's deep drive for self-preservation. The young people after all represent the future identity of the society concerned and that is why for example in some countries, the school day begins by saluting the national flag. Education is one of those subjects on which most people have opinions, partly because it is an aspect of socialization, the process by which a baby, who is a collection of biological urges, is turned into a law-abiding patriotic citizen. Youth Service claims public attention because it is seen in this light. The best chance of large grants from public funds is a widespread conviction that the young people are growing up out of sympathy with the cultural goals of their society, becoming delinquent and unpatriotic. And because organizers of youth work are ultimately dependent to some extent upon public support, they have to be aware of this scrutiny and from time to time examine their intentions and achievements:

they cannot operate in a vacuum. Education may help to create public opinion but it is also created by it.[1] 'Adolescents are the litmus-paper of a society':[2] they are among the first members of a community to be affected by rapid social change. Any organized provision for them will have to be, in the end, as responsive to the changes in social climate as the weather-vane to the wind.

'Youth' is often an emotional word for reasons of individual psychology. Among adults it can evoke feelings of envy 'because they have all their lives before them and ours are nearly over'. Older people's reactions to the young are often unconsciously conditioned because they are reminded too sharply of increasing years, fading powers and charm, and diminished opportunities. On the other hand, the sight of youth can evoke contrary feelings of pity since the observers see them stepping out with large hopes and optimistic plans not realizing through their inexperience, how painful pain can be, and how intractable injustice and evil. 'Youth' is one of the subjects on which middle-aged and elderly people are least likely to be able to think coolly and dispassionately: and 'What do *you* think about the young people of Britain today?' is one of the surest opening conversational gambits in most groups. The general public, as we shall see, are not well informed about Youth Service, but they have personal reasons for being deeply interested in anything that happens to the young. The architects of the provision are aware of this deep and abiding emotional response and are subject to its continuing pressure.

There is one other reason in society generally which relates to the constant reviews. Youth Service is avowedly a leisure-time provision and those responsible must constantly justify the effort and expense against a widespread conviction that 'people ought to pay for their own fun'. The many reviews are in part attempts to meet this demand, spoken and unspoken. For most enterprises which spend public and private money, there are measurable tests of success. A headmaster may quote the high number of children who go to grammar school from his school or the small number who appear in the Juvenile Court: an architect can point to his buildings: a medical officer of health gives an annual statistical survey. But those tangible criteria of success are harder to produce in Youth Service. Thus, to quote Douglas Hubery,[3] 'priority has always been given to the subject of training in right relationships', but it would be difficult to put the results of this attempt on paper from a year's working in a club. And because

c

the results are intangible, there is a tendency on the part of youth workers to justify themselves and what they do.

We have already trespassed upon the second set of reasons for constant revision, those in fact which spring from the Service itself. And certainly in recent years, doubts and misgivings about the work as a whole have increased the self-consciousness and the defensiveness of those who work within the Service. The full-time operatives have, not unnaturally, sought to provide a rationale for their profession. But there are reasons which come more directly and exclusively from within the Service itself.

One is that the total enterprise brings together so many and diverse partners. Everybody in a sense brings their own ideology to their work with young people, though the ideology is not always made explicit. Individually, there can be few endeavours in which a man's own private philosophy so clearly finds ultimate expression, though he may make a self-conscious effort to avoid this in the light of his professional ethics and training. There are powerful partners who are self-consciously committed to an interpretation of life's meaning, like the Boys' Brigade. Others are far more committed to a philosophy than they suppose. At one extreme, there are those who seem to see youth work primarily as a means of social control: by complete contrast there are those who seem to view it as a means of emancipating young people from an authoritarian society. Such major differences can be expected to lead to prolonged discussions.

Another fact is that the youth worker often finds himself at the meeting place of different, and even conflicting, expectations.[4] The general public may look to him to be say, a moral policeman whose work will diminish the incidence of youthful crime, noise and hooliganism: his employing body may well judge his work by the number of successes the club achieves in competitions and festivals or by how many members join evening classes of further education: the members themselves may expect him simply to be an organizer whose efforts lead to pleasurable experiences. He will also have expectations of himself, his own inner standards to judge his achievements. All four partners have a legitimate stake in the result. Reviews, examined carefully, are trying to see that all four receive their due.

But clearly the customer must come first and this brings us to the last reason. Youth Service is a voluntary activity in this country and likely to remain such: youth workers have no captive audience and if the youngsters do not like what is offered they can vote with their feet by staying away. Here, of course, lies the central dilemma. How can a publicly-supported service always give the youngsters what they want? Many are the twists and turns by which Youth Service seeks to be attractive to teenagers, whilst at the same time satisfying the general public that it is communicating socially-acceptable values. A further difficulty about meeting the tastes of the customers is that those tastes change rapidly. No sooner are, say, coffee bars installed than coffee bars are out of fashion. But the effort must be made. Youth Service cannot afford to be out-of-date (though it may, of course, help young people to discover new interests for themselves). And that is one of the reasons why it is always being passed under review since it is haunted by the possibility, at least at the level of the planners, of trying to meet the needs of today with the provision of yesterday.

What is written here may suggest that Youth Service has an impossible task and is in fact constantly running fast to maintain the same position. But only those will be in despair who think that tension is always to be deplored and joy is an absence of conflict. It is by the constant exploration of those issues, by all the partners concerned together, that we can begin to glimpse what should be and can be.

Notes:

1 c.f. S. Cotgrove, *The Science of Society*, Allen & Unwin, 1967, pp. 96–102 for the social functions of education.
2 Albemarle Report, p. 29.
3 D. S. Hubery, *Emancipation of Youth*, Epworth Press, 1963, p. 59.
4 This point is examined at greater length in the section, 'A cadre of professional workers', ch. 4.

3

The ten years after Albemarle

We have already observed that the Albemarle Report was unusual because a significant number of its practical recommendations were immediately implemented: we are now concerned to describe in more detail that part of the dream which came true during the ensuing decade.

To begin, more money was made available from two main sources—central government and local government.[1] The Department's annual grants have increased from £299,000 in 1959–1960 to £1·9 million in 1967–1968. They cover full-time training courses, headquarters expenses of national voluntary organizations for administration and training and grants to local voluntary capital projects. Local authority expenditure has shown a comparable increase from £2·58 million in 1957–1958 for England and Wales to £10 million in 1967–1968.

These simple facts about money represent a bigger commitment to Youth Service and enlarged opportunities. They relate closely to two points made in the Albemarle Report. The first was the disclosure of the small amount spent in this way in 1957–1958 by the Ministry and authorities combined,[2] £2¾ million, said to be less than the sum spent by the populace in the same year on fireworks. 'Of every pound they (Ministry and authorities) spent on education about 1d went on the Youth Service.' The other was the disclosure of the enormous variations in authority spending in this way. The notorious 'league table about youth work' shows that one authority spent 53s. per adolescent in the community and two others 1s. 6d. per adolescent. Though these figures are not completely reliable, since the basis of their compilation is imprecise, yet, that the disparities reveal differences of commitment to the Service is clear by other related facts. When the same questions were asked of the authorities in 1968, not only had overall expenditure increased nearly fourfold but there were

22

more leaders, full-time and part-time and the total number of youth groups assisted had increased by 112 per cent.[3]

The building programme was enormously expanded during the next few years though there has never been enough money for all the schemes submitted and a system of priorities is worked out nationally and locally. Building programmes for the period April 1960 to March 1968 allowed a start to be made on projects totalling £28 million—covering 3,000 schemes, both statutory and voluntary. At the same time, 60 youth sport projects totalling about £2½ million were programmed.

Albemarle complained of 'dingy drab premises': many of these remain but there are also modern buildings which represent a marked improvement and help to give a new impression of the intention of the Service. A landmark in the progress was the creation of a purpose-built youth centre on the Withywood housing estate in Bristol—a result of the work of the Development Group in the Architects' Branch at the Ministry.

No less important were the developments in the allied fields of training of leaders and the establishment of the profession of the full-time leader on a more satisfactory basis. As to the second, there was formed a joint negotiating committee with representatives for both employers and employees and representatives of the teachers' associations. Their annual reports setting out criteria of qualifications, salary scales and conditions of appointment, have been adopted.

Progress in training arrangements was on several levels. First, there was to be grant-aid for thirty students at Westhill College (subsequently raised to 74 including 14 community centre wardens): and the course at Swansea University, the N.A.B.C. course at Liverpool and the Y.M.C.A. course in London were recognized for qualification. But the largest development in this field was the opening of the National College at Leicester. It was to be an emergency course of one year and offered to candidates over 23. During the extended life of the college of nine years, there has not been a shortage of mature students for the course. The intention of the training at Leicester has followed closely the ideals laid down in the Albemarle Report with an emphasis upon social group method.[4] 'This practical work will, we hope, include regular experience in local group leadership under supervision, with opportunities for real responsibility, as well as visits of observation to different kinds of youth groups.' If the old distinction is valid, the youth worker at Leicester has been seen as a social worker rather than an educationist. Though today more would be in general agreement that a one-year course is seriously inadequate and that in any case, youth leaders should probably not be trained in isolation from other community workers, 'Leicester' plays an important part in the expansion of the Service being the biggest single factor in raising the numbers in the profession from 700 in 1961 to 1,500 in 1968. (Deeper issues raised by the growth of the profession are examined later.)

Another innovation in the same area was the establishment of 'optional youth courses' at teacher training colleges (now, colleges of education). This related to a view in Albemarle—'We have said that we regard the qualified teacher as the main source of recruitment.'[5] The introduction of a third-year-course for teachers facilitated the offer of an additional course of training in youth leadership. Eleven colleges were each permitted to take ten students in each of two years.[6] There were differences relating to content of course, which department of the college was responsible, amount of time devoted to the subject and whether the course carried an endorsement of the teacher's certificate. But the colleges were in consultation from the beginning and sought to share ideas and work out a common philosophy. Today there are about fifty colleges of education offering such courses and the issues that have been raised by this experience and development are the subject of later examination.

An important stage suggested in Albemarle was the setting up, by the Minister in July 1961, of a working party under the chairmanship of Mr G. S. Bessey to consider the nature of appropriate training for part-time youth leaders and assistants, both paid and voluntary. The report[7] stressed the need for the recognition of a minimum professional skill and the effective co-operation of statutory and voluntary agencies in the provision of joint training courses. A few years later, the Review Committee of the Youth Service Development Council was able to assess the impact of 'Bessey'.[8] The findings were significant: by the end of 1963, out of 146 L.E.As. in England and Wales, 110 had set up a joint training agency. They felt however that there were still in many areas major hindrances to full co-operation. The Report went on to argue for training for sensitivity, using group tutorial methods. These two reports, and even more the response to them in the country, have been among the most significant events in Youth Service in the 1960s, not primarily in the partnership involved but in the widespread dissemination through the country of more modern and effective ways of seeing the role of the youth worker and the appropriate form of his training. Today there are less and less of the 'talkie-talkie' kind of sessions where students sit in serried ranks and have information passed to them with perhaps a demonstration: and there are more and more courses where the aim is to increase the student's understanding and working skill by his more active participation in his own training.[9]

The Youth Service Development Council was set up immediately after the issue of the Report, though part of its work receives consideration in a later section, since it could not possibly be anticipated in 1960. But the Council has become the means—through its duty to 'advise the Minister'—of putting into effect some of the plans of Albemarle. Thus it was able to encourage and support experiments and research, two features which cannot be separated since new pieces of work are designed to provide information from which can come a better understanding of young people and an appreciation of the best ways of helping them. The list of pioneer efforts is too long to find a place here though it may be said that it includes much publicized efforts like the N.A.Y.C. project among the unattached and the Paddington Y.W.C.A. coffee bar experiment.[10] To date, 15 of these pioneering efforts among the 14s to 20s have been completed and 14 are still in progress. The subjects included the special needs of the handicapped (a feature which has received special attention since Albemarle, though still not enough) adventurous pursuits, voluntary service and training.

Three major pieces of research have been commissioned. A project from the University of Keele is examining the whole nature and purpose of youth work and the contrasting perceptions of people involved, both providers and clients. The University of Leeds has been asked to undertake research into the relationship between statutory and voluntary bodies. And the Government Social Survey is undertaking a study to explore three questions: first, who takes part at present in the activities of Youth Services: second, what are the differences between those who do and those who do not take part in those activities: third, what form of Youth Service can best meet the needs of young people.

A feature of the pioneering enterprises mentioned above was the co-operation of the national voluntary organizations. This is only one example of a new climate of co-operation after Albemarle, partly due to the improved grants position. Prior to Albemarle, the voluntary organizations had been taking stock of themselves and examining their methods and the Report encouraged them to go further. They were able to increase their staff: for example, it was at this time that the Church of England Youth Council set out to secure the appointment of a youth chaplain in every diocese. There were a number of promising developments and interesting pieces of specialized work. Welfare work was undertaken in rural Greece by a party of Rangers. The 'Teen' bar in Heeley, Sheffield attracted national interest. A group of N.A.B.C. clubs undertook the rehabilitation of Drake's Island near the south coast.

After the transfusion, new blood was coursing through the veins of Youth Service and the patient made at least a partial recovery and showed some signs of future robust health. We have seen in this section what of Albemarle came to pass: in some respects, the members of the Albemarle Committee builded even better than they knew: in others, no answers were found to the issues they raised and their dreams never came true: and new issues arose which they could not reasonably be expected to foresee.

HOPES DEFERRED

Considerable achievements have been outlined in the last section, yet predictably not all the hopes were fulfilled. Albemarle has not lacked critics. Some thought it was tied to assumptions of paternalistic control of the young by older people in the community; others thought by planning the extension of the work of buildings and organizations, it tended in its efforts to segregate adolescents from the total community. Yet others have expressed misgivings. not so much about the contents of the report, as its results. An extreme view here has been that since the issue of the Albemarle we have in Youth Service been spending more and more money on less and less members.

There is substance in each of these complaints, but they need to be balanced by contrary evidence. What we may perhaps say is that the Albemarle Report achieved its immediate objectives but in the end fell short of its long-term goals: the practical decisions were taken at once, but they by no means had the hoped-for effects. Several areas of enquiry demonstrate this result.

Thus the report planned for a deeper involvement of the general public in the affairs of the young. 'We believe that it is of the first importance that those gaps and those needs should be understood, not only by those directly concerned with the Youth Service but by society as a whole.'[11] Their one practical proposal in this area recommended the setting up of supporters' clubs. 'The importance of a good lively management committee to the life of a club hardly needs stressing, but we should like to see clubs associated with the life of their neighbourhoods through the creation of supporters' councils, which would have no direct share in the control of running the clubs, but would interpret the needs of the clubs to the neighbourhood and of the neighbourhoods to the clubs.'[12] Since 1960 not only has there been no significant response to this call but the training and education of members of management committees remains one of the urgent tasks of the Service, though there are examples of excellent committees and the majority of members are devoted and sincere.

Again, the Albemarle Report showed itself sensitive to the needs of the 'unattached'. '. . . there are others who find it difficult to come to terms with society and whose social incapacity can take many forms, from shyness to compulsive exhibitionism and crime. The Youth Service is there to help them, too, but at present this group is found principally among the "unattached".'[13] The remainder of the paragraph is devoted to a realistic assessment of the difficulties of eliciting a response from this social group. It may be argued that Youth Service is not equipped to cope with this type of youngster: partly because of its heavy reliance upon voluntary workers and because training for professionals has to be of a general nature at present with only a small element of casework. But what cannot be denied is that there has been no impressive improvement in this respect since the issue of the Albemarle Report. Clubs, for example, continue to cater largely for those who are reasonably well adjusted to their society: their commonest customers are the brighter 14 to 16 year old from secondary modern schools: the 'unattached' continue to view youth organizations as the childish provision offered by Establishment figures. The one or two exciting experiments in work among the 'unattached' have been widely admired, but not widely emulated: there are a few areas in which the detached street worker operates.[14]

Finally, there was a part of the vision which saw young people as far more active partners in the enterprise.

We should like to see more responsibility for activities and programmes turned over to the young wherever this can be made possible and real and the actual charge of things within their

27

compass (or just enough outside it to make them stretch
their minds) given to them.[15]

Youth leaders themselves often expect to frame the programme
for the young, and to coax them into support of activities
already decided. If they find that this does not work, they may
then allow members to enjoy the purely social activities of
the club without any strings attached. This too can lead to a
dusty boredom. The middle way, to encourage groups of friends
to work out their own programme within the shelter of a club,
can help to create the new spirit needed.[16]

Upon which the comment must be that though a few changes were
to come, partly under the pressure of a growing independence of
young people themselves, yet the words look optimistic now: there
were not great improvements in the self determination of youth groups
and the flexibility of their programmes: most groups went on doing
things in the same way which means adults largely deciding what to
suggest and organize, though their control may be disguised.

This is well-illustrated in a development that was heartening and
encouraging in the 60s and that merits a section on its own; the growth
of voluntary community work by young people.[17] Considerable work
has been done in this field by International Voluntary Service, Community Service Volunteers and Task Force. Of course, it is encouraging to see any group of people giving their time and energy to meeting
the needs of others without payment: a compassionate society will
continue to have a large dependence on voluntary effort: and if it is
young people who are serving others, we may reflect that this can be
a valuable part of their own emotional development away from the
egocentricity of childhood to the maturity of an adult who can feel
for others. But it is hard to escape the suspicion that in some cases,
at least, young people have been too much influenced in their choices
of a form of service by the adults concerned: not always have they
been asked to review the needs of a community and organize themselves to meet those needs. The possibilities of self-programming and
self-determination in community service have not been fully explored
and exploited. The new report found it necessary to say on this subject,
'We would like future developments to ensure maximum responsibility
for the young people concerned.'[18]

All of which only means that the Albemarle Report failed understandably to produce the ideal conditions for a Youth Service in which, to anticipate the argument, adolescents gain maximum freedom with maximum responsibility, and the support and fun which go along with those lofty aims.

UNEXPECTED DEVELOPMENTS

The Albemarle Report applauded the links between Youth Service and more formal aspects of education, like schools and colleges of Further Education. '. . . we envisage that the dual use of some schools will be a permanent feature of the Youth Service.'[19] 'It is . . . a mistake to attempt to draw too fine a distinction between recreation and the more formal kinds of further education.'[20] In view of what happened in the next few years, these were prophetic words though it is doubtful whether the scale of the development could have been anticipated in 1960. In a sense, during the decade under review, Youth Service, its philosophy and methods, began to invade the citadels of structured education. The growth of school-based youth clubs during this period is most marked and only less so is the use of the more informal methods of Youth Service in the school curriculum.

One measure of the progress is the number of joint appointments which had been made by the end of 1967—500 in fact. (The phrase 'joint appointments' covers a number of professional educational roles where part of the duties is to work with a youth group.) Of these, 300 are directly connected with schools, where the responsibilities are split between teaching in the class room and working in the club on school premises. There is a difficulty about titles in a new role but 'teacher-leaders' has been used to describe those who carry both teaching and youth leadership responsibilities and 'youth tutors' for those who develop youth work approaches in the school and carry them forward as leisure provision for those who have left school. There are many variations on this central theme: the commonest is the split between teaching and youth work though other variations bring in careers' guidance, counselling and Further Education. About 250 of the appointments are attached to secondary schools, most of them occupied by qualified teachers but qualified youth leaders account for a quarter of them. The remaining 200 joint appointments cover a wide range including the lecturer in a college of Further Education who leads a youth club.[21]

There is a general desire among educationists to see a further expansion in this realm, not excluding the Further Education field. It has been estimated that 1975 will show a threefold increase in the appointments with direct school connections and a doubling of the total for all joint appointments.[22]

The figures of workers involved represent a development of field work, particularly in schools, in two ways. First, there has been a big expansion of the number of youth organizations attached to schools—the nature of the attachment may vary—catering not only for those still at school but for those who have left. This is one of the ways in which Youth Service has come closer to schools. For example, the Duke of Edinburgh Award Scheme was never intended for those still at school, but it has flourished in many schools. Second, there has been the adoption in some schools of Youth Service methods of informality, participation and a measure of self-government. How far this change has gone and how many schools have participated, is a matter of current debate. Some say that the vast majority of schools are still ruled by didactic and authoritarian methods and therefore an effective Youth Service is needed by many adolescents outside school for their social education: others affirm that the changes are coming rapidly and that the social education of the 16s and under can largely be left to the schools.

Many factors have contributed to this change and it would be unfair to suggest that an Albemarle-inspired Youth Service has been the only or even the main influence; though a good case can be made for the argument that Youth Service has contributed to the development of structured education in much the same way that the Voluntary Schools contributed to the thinking and practice of the State Schools.

First, there was a practical aspect. 'Youth Service in schools' was one way of making the fullest use of resources that were in short supply. The school may be used if there is no youth centre. And who better than teachers to work with young people when trained and efficient leaders are in short supply?

But the changes reach further back to thinking about the purpose of education itself and its methods, and to a related question about the proper place of the school, and other educational institutions in the community.

This thinking began at least as far back as the Hadow report of 1941:[23] 'But in every case the aim of the teacher should be to help the pupils to organize as many of the out-of-school activities as possible, and to carry as much responsibility as is compatible with their age and experience.' Twenty-three years later, the Newsom Report[24] asks for the closest possible liaison between Youth Service and the schools and argues for approaches in the schools that have become dear to the heart of the youth worker—informal methods, projects and a bigger share for the youngster in his own process of education.

Between these two reports lie the work of many researchers and the issue of many documents generally in favour of more active forms of education, which they say, is not primarily about the ability to pass examinations, but more about personal development as a social being.[25] Many educationists would refute the terms 'formal education' as a description of what takes place in the better modern schools. 'The need to innovate on curriculum matters and make learning a personal activity is being acted upon by a rapidly increasing number of schools. Youth workers should not underestimate the speed with which changes in this direction are beginning to take place. Informal approaches of learning, once the preserve of the primary school and of Youth Service, are increasingly used in secondary schools and will provide common ground for the exchange of ideas and experiences between secondary school teachers and youth workers.'[26]

There has been a two-way traffic between these new, less didactic approaches and the colleges of education. In one direction a decided, though small, contribution has been made to the process by the hundreds of teachers who have now taken optional youth courses during their training; the evidence is that the study and practice of informal methods have improved their practice in the school. In the opposite direction, there has been a stronger pressure that training courses for teachers should fit them for these new approaches to learning: this is evidenced not only in preparation for less didactic methods in the classroom but in the demand for sociology to be added to developmental psychology on the curriculum (that they may better understand the background of those they teach) and in the slow growth of group methods and casework methods in the training of teachers.[27]

All of which, of course, has added significance in view of the raising of the school-leaving age to 16 in 1972–1973, for the new approach to learning is believed to be a more adult approach.

Related to these changes in the theory and practice of education was the appearance of a new answer to the question 'What is a school? (or evening institute/college of further education?)' And the

31

answer was to see them as part of the community, not segregated buildings reserved for the use of those compelled by law to attend them during set hours. This again was more than a comprehensive use of limited resources, but a conviction with several strands: that education is a lifelong process: that it takes place in association with others: that it should never unnecessarily segregate age-groups: that one respectable aim of education is community development. 'All new educational buildings should be viewed against a community setting. Where necessary, all new secondary schools (primary also, in rural areas) and colleges of further education should have social and cultural blocks designed for community (youth and adult) as well as student use,' says a memorandum from the Association of Liberal Education. There has been an increase in the multi-purpose usages of educational buildings with village and community colleges and community centres leading the way.[28]

These general changes have not been without their critics. For some, they fail to stress standards of excellence in learning: at the other extreme, for others they fail to take account of the special needs of adolescents, and this may indeed be a weakness of a more comprehensive approach. But it is easy to rejoice when one sees some of the examples of these developments in a particular place: school premises being used for people of all ages: young and old having their specialized activities in different parts of the same building, coming together over coffee, joining in common activities and going home together on the bus: youngsters who join an activity group in a youth club and then move to an advanced course in the subject in a college of further education, all on the same campus: a community complex where the people themselves provided the swimming pool: community complexes which include the public library: colleges of further education which offer sophisticated social and recreation provision: youngsters in school who spend part of their lunch hour preparing for a Duke of Edinburgh award: teachers who meet, informally, in the school club, the youngsters they meet in the classroom and whose teaching skill is thereby enhanced, not diminished: schools with a varied programme of extra-curriculum projects: schools which welcome voluntary organizations on to their premises as partners.

It is not everything we hope for: it is not even happening everywhere; but what is happening represents a marked advance from the days when Albemarle expressed a hope for links between the educational providers.

UNEXPECTED ISSUES

Growth brings new problems as well as fresh possibilities and it was to be expected that the expansion of the Youth Service after Albemarle would raise issues and create dilemmas which could not be wholly anticipated at the time. Some of those are dealt with elsewhere in this book: for example, the expansion of a school-based Youth Service gave rise to an argument about how much in fact should go on outside schools. But there is one issue which claimed a lot of attention and to which many of the other issues were directly related: the role and status of the professional youth worker.

The difficulties likely to arise from a large increase in the number of full-time youth leaders was referred to in Albemarle. 'We have concluded, as have many others, that full-time youth leadership is a life-long career for only a few. It would not be fair to attract intelligent men and women into this work unless we made it easy for them to move across to other professional work in education or the social services.'[29] They offer a solution. The qualified teacher should be the main source of recruitment: others, 'mature persons with a natural gift for leadership', should have the possibility of further training for a transfer to different educational and social work roles. It is true of course, that in the lives of many full-time youth leaders there comes a time when they feel too old for active work with a youth group: not all of them can or wish to move to administrative or training posts in Youth Service; but Albemarle here reveals the inherent difficulties of the position of the full-time youth leader's position in our society. There are not as yet many professions where at the training stage, plans have to be made for transfer to another occupation. Nor was the Albemarle solution everywhere feasible due to developments which we now consider.

The sudden growth in the number of full-time youth leaders meant inevitably that there were a number of people who were concerned about their status: they were organized into a professional body, the Youth Service Association, committed to arguing for conditions of service and the recognition of their expertise. The argument was likely to be 'A Youth Leader is a Youth Leader not an embryonic teacher or social worker: his training fits him to do what cannot be done without his training': which is only to say that the development of the profession followed a normal pattern.

Both the Parr[30] and Milson[31] researches showed that mature candidates for full-time youth leadership courses included a high percentage who in this choice were moving above the social class of their fathers, judged by occupation. It is difficult to see how anything else was possible, since the Leicester course, for example, was for the over 23s and the formal 5 G.C.E. 'O' levels for entry were by no means rigidly insisted upon. The college was not likely to be overwhelmed by applications from folk established in their jobs, graduates say, especially in view of the admittedly poor salary scales and uncertain career prospects.

One answer often given is 'the saints and heroes' solution. Youth leaders are here expected to do their work without thought of their own future and the provision for their families. This is a rare expectation, and though we hold strongly that nobody can go on happily being a full-time youth leader unless he retains a sense of vocation and a streak of idealism, yet to rely on this completely is an unrealistic and out-moded rubric, in process of being abandoned in our society even for nurses. Parr found that full-time youth leaders were likely to begin with a sense of vocation and idealistic standards, though this tended to diminish in the light of professional considerations under pressure of family needs: workers in voluntary organizations were likely to retain their idealism longer than those who worked for statutory agencies.

Fundamentally the problem arises because the full-time youth leader is a 'marginal man' uneasily poised between education and social work. Hence there is for him a large area of 'role ambiguity'. Milson found that there were in fact different styles of role-performance, but these were decided, not so much by the forms of training or the expectation of employers or clients, as by the personality traits and social experiences of the leaders themselves.

'What is a full-time youth leader supposed to do?' is not a question to which the majority of the public could give an informed answer and so his work often lacks the support of general definition. There are those who see him as an unfortunate phenomenon since he inevitably represents adult control of the young. Others find him harmless enough but see no place for Youth Service as a whole sandwiched between other educational and social work provision. His own professional ethic tells him that he should work himself out of a job since he may be considered to be a success when the young people no longer need him.

Though he may wish to be client-orientated and put the service to young people above every personal and professional consideration, in some cases at least, he cannot help viewing as a threat developments like school club work, which appear to squeeze out his expertise. The raising of the school leaving age to 16 may appear to take away part of his constituency. If he was everywhere welcomed in schools, his response might be different but this is not so: as a worker with perhaps one year's emergency training, with less academic qualifications, he is not universally accorded parity of esteem with teachers. (Of the 1,500 full-time youth leaders in 1969, it is probably true to say that more than 1,000 of them were emergency trained.)

Moreover, the official expectations of the full-time youth leader are likely to change with the changing philosophy about Youth Service. For example, the current stress is upon the full-time youth worker as a community development worker, but this came too late to be included in the training of the vast majority.

Nor was there any fulfilment of Albemarle hopes about facilities for further training to transfer to another role: a few have become teachers after shortened courses, a few have become social workers. But there has been no organized system of further training and transfer. Moreover, perhaps most of the transfers can be traced to disappointment rather than increasing years.

The increase in the number of full-time workers facilitated by Albemarle was a large contribution to the growth of the Service: but it raised questions whose breadth, intensity and complexity were not, and perhaps, could not be anticipated at the time.

Later, we look at possible solutions which include new forms of training.

IS ALBEMARLE OUT OF DATE?

It would be strange if, ten years after its issue, the Albemarle Report was in every way relevant to the needs of young people today. We live at a time of rapid social change and the young are among the members of the community most vulnerable to the effects of rapid social change. In some ways, the Report was uncannily prophetic: it not only indicated important features of twentieth century Britain, but it introduced issues which have become crucial. Yet to read parts of the report today is to realize how much change there has been in ten years, particularly in the social position of young people; the omissions are more striking than the inclusions; Albemarle related to a world where drug-taking by the young, students' revolt and coloured immigrants were not subjects of abiding public concern.

One can in fact, work through Chapter 2 ('Young people Today')[32] and divide the issues there raised into different categories of their rating ten years later.

1 Issues which are still with us and unresolved, for example, the changing pattern of women's lives or delinquency.

2 Issues which have diminished in importance, for example, the ending of National Service.

3 Issues which have become more important, such as the rejection by young people of the norms commonly accepted by older people. 'A particularly imaginative effort is needed by anyone over 35—by middle-class parents as much as by working-class parents—to understand the true quality of the lives of this generation which is itself so often "classless" in appearance, and in some of its habits.'

4 Issues which were not, and perhaps could not be, anticipated by the Albemarle committee, such as those created by the growing number of young coloured citizens of Britain. This became the subject of an enquiry by a committee set up by the Youth Service Development Council.[33]

There is plenty of evidence here to argue for the need to take a fresh look at the Service in the light of our previous point that effective youth work always keeps close to the social situation. And to be fair, Albemarle planned only for ten years, though it proved to be a defect that it was largely dedicated to the expansion of traditional methods and provision.

Perhaps there are a few generalizations which describe the changed position of young people in our society though none of them can be put forward without considerable qualification.

a More opportunity

The Albemarle Report, whilst recognizing continuing difficulties in education, summarized solid gains. '. . . both secondary and technical education are in process of being widely expanded and improved: opportunities are increasing for those boys and girls who do not go to grammar schools: many schools and colleges of further education are broadening their concepts of study: social education and physical recreation are receiving more attention.'[34] On the whole it may be said that those processes have gathered momentum, though admittedly in planning and hopes more conspicuously than in achievement. Since 1960 a lot of water has flowed under the educational bridge and much of it designed to help the average youngster, like the Industrial Training Act.

> We have had the Newsom and Plowden Reports; the Schools Council was established in 1964; the Government has pursued its policy of abolishing separatism in secondary education linked with the abolition of examination pressures at 11 : the Certificate of Secondary Education was introduced for secondary school pupils who are not in the highest range of academic ability; the training of teachers has been lengthened; school buildings are being designed to take account of the changed approaches to learning and their use by both school and community; a wide variety of new teaching aids and media are being used increasingly and a National Council for Educational Technology has been established.[35]

There are some observable effects for example in the increased number of young people on day-release courses and the fact that over 50 per cent of young people stay on at school beyond the statutory age for leaving. There are still gross inequalities and lack of educational opportunity; the vast disparity in social and recreational provision for those who are recruited for higher education and those who are not, continues. But the decade has seen large opportunities in many ways offered to more young people in Britain.

b Further alienation

This may be too strong a word and 'independence' should be preferred. For it is all too easy from much publicized accounts of students' revolts at one end of the scale, and growing hooliganism and violent youthful crime at the other, to gather an impression that a whole generation has rejected their society. Careful research suggests that a dull conformity among the young is commoner than an urgent radicalism.[36] Many adults, for example, picture young people as being wildly promiscuous in their sexual activity, but Michael Schofield's careful enquiries do not support this view.[37] But certainly the revolt of the young is more vocal and spectacular today and it relates to a demand among perhaps a small but growing section of the populace, that ordinary citizens should have more say in decisions which affect their lives. There are other features of the relative independence of young people today which are linked not so much perhaps with generational tension, as to the fact that the young think of themselves as adults at an earlier age: and in the end, society has to make concessions and lower the age of social maturity. Earlier marriage is one; another is the expansion of 'teenage culture' which, though the term has been questioned, refers to a style of life, a set of cultural values—including music, ethics, dress and hair styles—associated with the adolescent age-group.

c Deeper need

There is evidence that the condition of a modern society like ours—increasingly urbanized and mobile, fast-changing, meritocratic, anomic—places an increasing number of youngsters, though still a minority, at risk. 'Rootless in Cities'[38] demonstrates that there is a growing number of young people who are adrift and in urgent need of pastoral care of a specialized kind. Clegg and Megson, working in the West Riding of Yorkshire, estimated that though 2% of children receive help from special agencies—psychiatric, social, medical—another 12% need such help but do not receive it.[39] There are many signs of the truth in this proposition: growth of drug-taking amongst the young: growth of hooliganism, vandalism and violent crime: the need for and the response to counselling services for the young, in universities no less than in poor areas of our cities; the problems of the coloured teenager.

In seeking to estimate the needs of a significant section of our youth population at a time like this, the new report gives a long list beginning with adult support and guidance and learning how to accept responsibility in the community (para. 66).[40]

Do slogans have a value in Youth Service? Did 'association, training and challenge' help or hinder thinking about the possibilities? If the answer is 'Yes', then in the changed conditions of our time, the aims of Youth Service might be to provide opportunities for 'fun, interests, counselling and participation'.

Notes:

1 *Youth and Community Work in the 70s*, H.M.S.O., 1969, paras. 25 and 26.

2   Albemarle Report, p. 8.
3   *Youth and Community Work in the 70s*, para. 26.
4   Albemarle Report, p. 75. c.f. also Appendix II.
5   Albemarle Report, p. 74.
6   They were: Chelsea College of Physical Education
                Culham College
                Dartford College of Physical Education
                Edge Hill College
                Kenton Lodge College
                Kesteven Training College
                Mount Pleasant Training College
                Newland Park Training College
                City of Portsmouth College
                Swansea Teacher Training College
                Westhill College
7   *The Training of Part-time Youth Leaders and Assistants,*
    H.M.S.O., 1962.
8   c.f. *A Second Report on the Training of Part-time Youth Leaders
    and Assistants,* 1965.
9   c.f. Mary Morse, *The Unattached*, Pelican, 1965.
10 c.f. G. Goetschius and J. Tash, *Working with Unattached Youth*,
    Routledge & Kegan Paul, 1967.
11 Albemarle Report, p. 41.
12 ibid., p. 48.
13 ibid., p. 105.
14 Including London and Liverpool.
15 Albemarle Report, p. 49.
16 ibid., p. 56.
17 c.f. *Service by Youth*, H.M.S.O., 1966; also M. and A. Dickson,
    Count Us in, Dobson, 1967.
18 *Youth and Community Work in the 70s*, H.M.S.O., para. 246.
19 Albemarle Report, p. 66.
20 ibid., p. 103.
21 For this section I am indebted to *Youth and Community Work
    in the 70s*, paras. 280–84.
22 ibid., para. 279.
23 *The Education of the Adolescent*, H.M.S.O., 1941.
24 *Half our Future*, H.M.S.O., 1963.
25 c.f. in particular the relevant reports of the Schools Council and
    in this field the work of the Nuffield Foundation.
26 *Youth and Community Work in the 70s*, para. 52.
27 At least two Colleges of Education are offering an introduction
    to casework skills—Edge Hill and Westhill.
28 *Youth and Community Work in the 70s*, para. 269.
29 Albemarle Report, p. 72.
30 T. J. Parr, *The Role and Professional Identity of Youth Leaders
    in Statutory and Voluntary Organizations,* unpublished M. Ed.
    thesis, Manchester University, 1969.

31 F. W. Milson, *Full Time Youth Leaders in the Midlands*, unpublished Ph.D thesis, Birmingham University, 1966.
32 Albemarle Report, p. 31.
33 The Hunt Committee, *Immigrants and the Youth Service*, H.M.S.O., 1967.
34 Albemarle Report, p. 22.
35 *Youth and Community Work in the 70s*, para. 51.
36 E. M. and M. Eppel, *Adolescents and Morality*, Routledge & Kegan Paul, 1966.
37 M. Schofield, *The Sexual Behaviour of Young People*, Longmans, 1965.
38 Published by the National Council of Social Service and the National Institution of Social Work Training, 1968.
39 *Children in Distress*, Pelican, 1968.
40 The full list can be read in paragraph 66 of *Youth and Community Work in the 70s*.

4

Gaps and growing points

WHAT ARE WE TRYING TO DO?

William Smith, the founder of the Boys' Brigade, included among his aims 'the promotion of habits of obedience, reverence, discipline, self-respect and all that tends towards true Christian manliness'.[1] The statement is characteristic of the pioneers and organizers of the Youth movements which sprang up in this country in the half-century from about 1860 onwards: these youth workers had clear, self-conscious aims.

They were able to make three assumptions which were not at the time widely questioned. The first was the belief system: these early movements were out to make more Christians. Each Boys' Brigade company for example was to be under the control of a church. Among phrases in the early literature of the Y.M.C.A. are 'Mutual edification and evangelization of young men' and 'The Association must not be considered as places of amusement for young people'. The second underlying assumption was that young people were to be taught to support the existing order of things. 'A scout is loyal and a scout obeys,' according to Baden-Powell. Towards the end of the eighteenth century, Hannah More had commended her plan for educating farm workers in the following words to the parishioners of Cheddar: 'I said I had a little plan which I hoped would secure their orchards from being robbed, their rabbits from being shot, their poultry from being stolen, and which might lower the poor-rates.'[2] And the accepted motives of youth work do not appear to have changed by the late nineteenth century. This was related to the third assumption namely that society knew how the individual ought to behave and that youth work could be one means of passing on the accepted ethical standards. At least youth workers were clear how working class folk ought to behave. 'The sooner we recognize that recreation unorganized is a danger, the better,' said Dr J. Scott Lidgett, in advocating the Wesley Guild in the Methodist Church.

From the vantage of the twentieth century, it is easy to poke fun at those citizens of another age. Bernard Shaw achieves this effectively in the comments of Undershaft in *Major Barbara*: 'Young ladies have little idea how much cottage girls value instrumental accompaniment to singing, so that if possible a piano should always be in the room. Tea, cake and bread-and-butter seem particularly to be elements of eating and drinking which can be used to the glory of God.' We have written deliberately of 'self-conscious' motives. In fact, as in most human situations, the aims would be more complex than was known: the unconscious motives included those that were both worse and better than the self-conscious motives. As to the first, Davies and Gibson point out that fear was involved: the privileged saw themselves under threat from the masses increasing in numbers and power: youth work was supported as social control, an aspect of 'educating our masters'. 'They dread the fermenting, in the populous cities, of some new, all-powerful explosive, destined one day to shatter into ruins all their desirable social order' (G. F. C. Masterman 1907). Another element was the need of existing voluntary movements, like churches, to survive by attracting new recruits. As the Archbishop of York put the matter in 1878, 'The Church of England must either come into contact with the working classes of the country, or else her national position will suffer and her leading position be ultimately lost.'[3] But mixed with these baser motives were more idealistic and compassionate intentions. One was *noblesse oblige*, the feeling that the privileged should serve the underprivileged. A familiar expression of this sentiment is in the statement of aims of the founders of the Ardwick Lads' Club. '(We) thought it incumbent on us, fortunately placed as we were, to do something to help those who had to spend their lives in the mean and sordid districts and slums of our city.' Again, as in many human enterprises, the practice of youth work, the close contact with young people, modified and to some extent, enriched the self-conscious motives. Religious enthusiasts developed an eye for the 'lesser pearls'. Of one of the most 'deeply spiritual' of early Y.W.C.A. workers, Miss Battersby, it was reported that she soon realized 'that young women have bodies as well as souls, and that their bodies as well as their souls have to be cared for'. We may briefly notice two other developments not obviously connected with the original self-conscious aims. One was the interest in the open air and the attempts to take city youngsters into the surrounding country-side. The other was the increasing emphasis upon the personal and individual development of the youngster.

The main purpose of this brief excursion into the recent history of British youth work, has been to throw into stronger relief the contrasted position of today. No longer present are the three assumptions which we saw were the basis of a clear self-conscious purpose of youth service. We cannot maintain a 'conversion' aim since ours is a society in which the Christian faith is only one of the options: the Churches in Britain operate more and more in a missionary situation: there is no longer a consensus of opinion which thinks it is a 'good thing' to be a Christian, though religious education is compulsory in State schools. Nor can conformity to the existing order of things be an adequate goal: youth workers cannot be expected to deliver the vote in favour of things as they are: we live at a time of rapid social change when the foundations of modern living are being re-examined. Similarly we witness a diminution of the area in which the behaviour of the individual is defined by the expectation of society. Many of the folksy sayings of a generation ago, enshrining the norms of conduct, sound ridiculous today. 'A woman's place is in the home', 'Children should be seen and not heard.' Youth Service cannot simply be a socializing agency teaching young people to do the 'right thing' because there is confusion about the 'right thing' in important areas of human conduct.

The new alignment has altered the relationships of older and younger in modern societies and has radical results in youth work. No longer are the older people seen as the guardians of an honoured tradition—in belief, standards and skills—which have to be learned by younger people. The simple clear-cut purpose of Youth Service has gone.

There are those who fight a rearguard action. They assume that the expression of the truth they have found is Absolute Truth to be accepted by everybody. They see the world in the light of their own ideology, whether it be a brand of Christian faith, a set of ethical principles, or an activity and skill which may be as diverse as boxing, drama or mountain-climbing. And though a few of those folk appear to have an invincible persistence, never doubting that what has proved decisive for them must be so for everybody else, not swerving from a path where they interpret the needs of others too exclusively in the light of their own—yet their clientele diminishes and more and more in Youth Service circles they are stigmatized as 'indoctrinators'. The philosophy and practice of the movement has swept past them unobserved.

It is now twenty years since Dr J. Macalister Brew wrote that in former times the youth leader said to the member, 'I will teach you': but his modern counterpart says, 'Let us learn together'. The Albemarle Report warned against an adult attitude which offered young people 'a packaged deal' of beliefs and standards.

One of the earliest examples (and most refreshing) of the new type of relationship to be developed in youth movements is provided by Alicia Percival.[4] Fifty Girl Guides were invited to a Royal Garden Party at Buckingham Palace in 1919. One Guide was a factory girl who had never been away from home. A lady visitor, seeing the girl in uniform, said: 'Fetch us some chairs, please—I expect that is what you are here for.' The girl answered, quite politely: 'Ah'm fain fer to get chairs aw reet, being as Ah'm a Guide, but Ah'm going to tell thee, Ah've been axed to this 'ere do same as thisel' and ah've as much right 'ere as thee.'

It is neither possible nor desirable to return to the old days, yet the new situation is not all gain: Youth Service suffers from the lack of a clear objective. Many things have happened in Youth Service in the last thirty years but there has not been a widespread radical appraisal and adjustment of aims to suit a new age. The infinite variety of methods used by the partners, is a source of enrichment, but the acknowledgement of a common primary goal would yield substantial improvement. Diversity can be carried to the point of fragmentation of effort. The consequences can be seen all too clearly. A few youth workers stagger on from one session to the next, not bothering about aims, like the club leader in *Eighty Thousand Adolescents*[5] asked by the researchers about his purpose. He replied by calling to his colleague in the next room, 'Bob, why do we run this club?' More workers experience a loss of confidence because they find themselves in a service which suffers from a confusion of aims. For years now, conferences connected with this branch of education have been dominated by the question 'What are we trying to do?' Others respond by an over-commitment to the values of the movement in which they are working: judge every proposition by the values of the Scouts or Guides or Brigades or one of the other associations: they serve an organization rather than young people. Among the general public, there are hopes that youth organizations will diminish juvenile delinquency, exercise social control over youngsters who step out of line and effectively deal with the 'youth problem'. But most youth workers would not be happy about this negative purpose.

Yet the dilemma remains. Youth Service would be strengthened by having an overall purpose but what can this be in a pluralistic society? There is less and less agreement about religious beliefs, ethical standards and social goals. Moreover, there are two tests of a feasible aim. One is it must be broad enough to fit the differing methods used by various movements: broad enough too to avoid any regimenting of young people. Occasionally, the youth work of contemporary Communist countries is quoted with approval by those who find aimless much of what is done in this country. True, the members of the Komsomol are usually found to be more socially responsible and politically informed than young people of the same age in Britain. But there is plenty of evidence that this has been achieved by a rigid control of their thinking which has not allowed them to consider the alternatives to Communist philosophy and economics. Deliberate complete and self-conscious indoctrination of the young is not one of the alternatives before us in Britain.

On the other hand, any stated aim must not be so broad as to prove vague and nebulous, a meaningless slogan rather than a standard of achievement. For a long time, the various youth movements in Britain were content to accept one shared aim: it was 'citizenship'. But this was interpreted so variously as to become meaningless: it made strange bedfellows of Girl Guides and Young Communists. There have been many slogans but few practical measuring-rods.

Short definitions are apt to be inaccurate: it is difficult to write the whole truth on a banner. Long definitions are cumbersome and not remembered. Despite these limitations, however, an attempt is made here to put forward for discussion, a basic aim for Youth Service: it is 'the critical involvement of young people in a society which seeks to be compassionate and participant'.

'Critical' relates to the fact that we ought no longer to expect young people to receive a tradition or to perpetuate an accepted social order: at a time of rapid social change, we need their ideas and energy. Older people in Britain today adopt a variety of attitudes to the rising generation.[6] They may be very critical of them; or they may fear them; or they may seek to emulate their fashions and style of life; they may ignore, patronize, exploit, indoctrinate or neglect them. But the creative attitude to the young in a society like ours is to see them as partners in the new form of living together which is emerging. They are not 'wonderful' neither are they 'hopeless', but they have immense promise as colleagues, called to define the social task as well as to share it. Youth workers of whatever kind—whether 'running' a

Scout troop or a Guide company, serving in a club canteen, managing a football team or engaged in one of a dozen other possible roles— are one organized expression of this ideal intention in our country. If there is any conflict between the generations in our country, it cannot be settled by more effective controls from one side: not even by arbitration: but only by the kind of integration which issues in common action after a full exchange of views. Behind its many forms this is what youth work should be doing and the measure of achievement in this area is the test of every local piece of youth work.

'Involvement' reminds us that though we abhor the totalitarian methods of dictatorship countries, we cannot afford to rear a nation of individualists. The democracies may not survive unless they can include social responsibility in their educational programmes. If regimentation is out, so is anarchy and nihilism. Fortunately there is no reason to suppose that young people will not serve a community which they help to make, in which their voice is truly heard; indeed, there is much encouraging evidence to suggest the contrary, namely that young people will give devoted service when they have a stake in the society. Perhaps Youth Service (in the sense of partnership between statutory and voluntary agencies) was unfortunate in the time of its birth: it came when before our eyes was the example of the Hitler Jugend and the Young Fascists and maybe we over-reacted against national purpose finding any place in the work.

'A society which seeks to be compassionate and participant'—is an attempt to provide a social philosophy, a scale of values which would command fairly wide acceptance. (Most people will surely agree that a community which cares is better than one which neglects and it is to be preferred that men should rule themselves whenever possible and not be ruled by others.) It should, for example, unite most humanists and most Christians, though obviously they would have different sanctions for their endeavours. A 'compassionate' society is one where need not merit is the qualification for help: a 'participant' society is one where more and more people are involved in the decisions which affect their lives; the first is a defence against meritocracy, the second against bureaucracy—twin evils of an industrial, technological, urbanized society. If it is argued that the two words simply mean 'democracy' or 'civilized living', we do not disagree but the first is a tired, over-used word and the second phrase is not commonly used. 'Compassionate and participant' is a candidate for the breadth and definiteness that has been seen to be a requirement.

To state the primary purpose in terms of social goals need not mean that the needs of individuals are overlooked. Mature and developed young men and young women, who have a breadth of interests and can enjoy many different experiences, are likely to be able to make a better contribution to their society. The Albemarle Report saw Youth Service as meeting the needs of young people for association, training and challenge: elsewhere, we have argued that, ten years later, this should now be for fun, interests, counselling and participation: these four relate both to individual development and social responsibility.

The foregoing discussion may appear theoretical and high-faluting to anybody engaged in the night-by-night running of a youth organization or who serves say on the management committee of a youth club. We have expressed our conviction of the value of a comprehensive purpose and the weakness which flows from a lack of this. We go on to claim there are homely and daily ways of expressing 'critical involvement in a society which seeks to be compassionate and participant'.

A leader who has time to listen to the personal problems of one member, though this may divert his attention from trophy-winning preparation, is giving, unconsciously, an object lesson in a compassionate society: a worker who refuses to decide issues for youngsters which they are capable of deciding for themselves—even though they want and expect him to decide for them—is saying more eloquently than any words can achieve that he believes in an open society: a member of a management committee who judges the work of the club, not by the successes in competitions or festivals but by the social and emotional development of the youngsters—a leader who organizes and encourages members and groups to be involved with the community outside, though he knows this may weaken the ties of loyalty to the organization in which he works—a worker in a uniformed organization who prefers questioning of the values and assumptions of the movement to blind uncritical acceptance of them—a councillor on an education committee who refuses to regard numbers attending as the sole criterion of success—all these, and many more in diverse ways, may be interpreting on the shop-floor, the maxim 'active involvement in a society that seeks to be compassionate and participant'. And though it will not always be easy to apply, we have at last a measure by which we may know success or failure.

Such a definition of aims would also have implications for the partnership of the various movements and agencies within Youth Service. It would be unfair to disregard the levels of co-operation already revealed: but it would be folly to deny that the partnership can be deepened and extended. (Later we consider practical sugges-tions for improvement.) Attempts to provide joint leadership courses have revealed tensions in some places. Conferences which bring together workers from different sections can sometimes uncover the need for a common language—or perhaps a second language. In the worst cases youth workers are seen to be living on an island which they will insist is the whole inhabited youth work world. Or to change the figure, they acknowledge only a 'State' law and not a 'Federal' law which is binding on all. An overall accepted objective would facilitate discussions in the key—'This is what we are doing to help our members to equip themselves to be critically involved in a society which seeks to be compassionate and participant.' It is only fair to add, however, that the acceptance of this aim would see an extension of youth work outside membership organizations and buildings into other types of association and into many places—a point that is later treated in greater detail.

No less important are the implications for training: and this applies to the preparation of both full-time and part-time leaders. We have seen elsewhere that many questions have been raised by the growth of a cadre of professional youth workers in the last ten years. They suffer from role uncertainty for a number of reasons: they work with several and occasionally opposing sanctions—the desires of the mem-bers, the expectations of their employers, the demands of law and order, their own professional standards. There has been confusion and a few have even argued that the youth worker should be non-judgmental! Part of this confusion arises from the lack of a clear objective in Youth Service itself. The case is not dissimilar with many voluntary and part-time workers. The writer has frequently interviewed, as part of an assessment process, students who have completed a Bessey-type training course. They find most difficulty in giving a satisfactory answer to questions like: 'What are we trying to do?', 'What is the purpose of youth work?' Perhaps they do not understand; the question is obscure. 'Well, what have you done on those nights when you have been in the club as part of your practical training?' 'Talked to people/been there/hung about/collected subscriptions.' This is no plea for an abandonment of the methods of informal educa-tion. Nor should people be too often self-consciously aware of their overall purpose: that would rob their service of valuable spontaneity. But can people be effective unless somewhere in their minds there is an accepted goal? Agreement on aim would help training since it would provide part of the answer to the important question, 'Training for what?'

Finally agreement on goals would help to create a better understanding of the Service among the general public. There are frequent complaints that there is little appreciation of the best intentions of youth movements. (This again is a subject to which we return.) Hence the work receives inadequate support. Recruits are not forthcoming to fill voluntary and professional positions. Or complaints are made that many people involved—councillors and members of management committees for example—do not understand what is at stake: they may have zeal without knowledge, be excellent people with limited objectives and vision.

The enthusiasts for Youth Service should ask themselves how far they are themselves to blame for a situation they deplore: can they expect to sell a product they are at a loss to describe?

A SERVICE FOR CHILDREN?

Officially, Youth Service provides leisure time activity for young people between the ages of 14 and 21. But it is generally believed that the overwhelming response is from the younger adolescents. After about 16 or 17 there is a marked falling off in the membership of youth organizations. Moreover, it is held that this tendency has become more emphatic in the last ten years; that the juvenile image has been stamped more firmly on Youth Service since the Albemarle Report (1960).

There are not enough reliable national statistics about youth organizations to prove the point beyond doubt from this source. Such figures are notoriously difficult to come by. Does one count membership or attendance? If the former, then their value is reduced by overlapping in membership; many boys of 14 and 15 for example belong to more than one organization. Again, by this method the member who attends once a month is added to the member who goes to club three times a week. Moreover, returning officers are tempted to exaggerate their figures to gain support and prestige. If attendance is counted, then does one count on the best attended night when say, the club dance is held or on the worst attended night, say the activities evening? Youth workers are familiar with the wild fluctuations in club

attendance, often from one night to the next, frequently quite inexplic-
able except that the bad nights always seem to coincide with the
advent of distinguished visitors and leave the worker explaining, 'We
are thin tonight. You ought to have visited us last night when we
were crowded out.'

A number of surveys have however been attempted.[7] One or two
of them have been on a national basis using a significant sample:
others have been undertaken locally. Both membership and attendance
have been counted. From these enquiries several trends appear which
support the general view that Youth Service is commonly seen as a
provision for the younger end of the official age group. The following
features are found most frequently:

1 Boys leave youth organizations at 17 and girls at 16.
2 In membership, the main involvement is the 13s to 16s and then
falls away rapidly.
3 Many of those who attend youth clubs are still at school and
aged 14 and 15.
4 Voluntary organizations, compared with statutory organizations,
attract a slightly higher proportion of the over 18's but both agencies
attract relatively few in this age range.

Workers in the field—youth leaders, full time and part time, further
education officers and the like—support these views from their
experience. Typical is the comment of the Derbyshire Education Committee. 'But enquiries are confirming that much of the existing provision, both in the field of youth and adult organizations, seem to
lack features which are of particular relevance to the expectations of
young adults, and that it is the absence of such features which may
at this time account for the disinclination of many young adults to
engage in community activities.'[8]

Since there are no figures for pre-1960, it is from this source—the
impressions of workers in the field—that the judgment arises of
Youth Service having less appeal for older teenagers in the past ten
years.

There are features in the organization of Youth Service itself which
have contributed to this situation.

One is that there has always been uncertainty about the exact age
group to be catered for and there have been several changes in the
official scale. Circular 1486, which began in November 1939 a partnership between statutory and voluntary agencies, stated explicitly that

the service was for those who had ceased full-time schooling, that is the over 14s. Had this ever been taken seriously and literally, it would have excluded grammar school youngsters of 15 and upwards. When after the war the school leaving age was raised, this restricted the provision again, officially, to those 15 and over. The Albemarle Report proposed a lowering of the age to 14 on the grounds that youth organizations could provide a useful bridge between school and work. They asked for the situation to be reviewed if and when the school leaving age was raised to 16.

In practice, these official pronouncements have had little effect upon the membership of youth organizations. Youngsters below the official age have always been welcomed and local authorities have grant aided organizations which were known to include among their members youngsters below the statutory age. But the changes and the uncertainty in official quarters have not helped to fix a clear picture in the mind of the general public. 'If the trumpet shall give an uncertain sound, who will follow?' The exact boundaries of the service have not been clear and this means that it will be seen as a service for the younger adolescents since this has been part of the history and the traditions of youth movements.

This leads to the second pressure from within the Service. The youth organizations best known to the public are those which, like the Scouts and the Boys' Brigade, include children among their members and in which indeed children usually predominate. The voluntary organizations are the older and, in many respects, they remain the stronger of the two partners. But they are not associated in the public mind with work among young adults. This view is supported by an analysis of their membership. The Standing Conference of National Voluntary Organizations was founded in 1936 by thirteen of the leading national voluntary movements. A condition of association was that the movement should have not less than 10,000 members between the ages of 14 and 20. Yet it included not a few the bulk of whose membership was schoolchildren. The public impression is confirmed by explicit statements from these agencies. 'It remains true that the Boys' Clubs exist for boys who want to belong regardless of whether or not they are still at school.'

The voluntary organizations are not unaware that they have a 'juvenile image' for the public. They have made strenuous efforts in recent years to show that they realize that the age of social adulthood has changed; that the different needs of younger and older teenagers can be met in their movement. Several have issued reports[9] giving a 'new look' to the organization, essaying the difficult task of adjusting to the times but retaining their traditional identity; hoping thus to satisfy the 'Old Guard' of the movement and yet attract new customers. The report from the N.A.B.C. quoted above admitted that the greater the membership in a unit of those under 14, the greater the likelihood of wastage among the over 14s. It remains to be seen whether these efforts will succeed in convincing the community that youth movements are for young adults.

Another pressure, in the present discussion, comes from the growth of school-based youth service during the past few years. This has taken several forms. Youth wings have been added to existing school premises; the 'community school' has been built which makes provisions for all age groups; some schools have included club programmes as part of their curriculum or for out of school hours; youth tutors have been appointed in many places with dual responsibility for teaching in the school and leading in the club. One authority has developed youth associations in school buildings providing for those at and those who have left school and often counting a membership of over 500. Without doubt, the growth of school based youth service is one of the marked features of the last few years.

There are many advantages about this arrangement. It makes possible the joint use of resources, both human and physical; is an example of comprehensive planning of education in an authority's area and serves to link school and youth work with the rest of the community. At present however a school-based youth service emphasizes its juvenile image. Commonly, when youth work takes place in a school, it is seen as a provision for children rather than for young adults. In particular it is likely to be this for school leavers who often want to have done with school, at least for the time, being who see it as the place and the symbol of an earlier stage in their growth and status. Progressive educationists often say that the school is beginning to have a different public identity, as a 'community complex' offering educational opportunity of different types and to all age groups: they quote examples of where the change has taken place.[10] But it may be doubted how far this process of re-identification has gone. Still for the vast majority, a 'school' is a place attended by children and this description affects the way in which youth work in schools is seen.

In addition to the factors within Youth Service itself, there have been, during the past few years, changes in the social position of young people in Britain which have helped to make the Service look juvenile. Briefly, it may be said, that young people have, during this period, gained adult status at an earlier age: since 1 January 1970, this is recognized at law: from that date the age of majority has been 18.

British writers on the sociology and psychology of youth have often complained that young people were accorded 'graded recognition' of their social maturity.[11] At what age is the teenager recognized to be an adult? The answer for a long time depended on which particular aspect of adult behaviour the questioner had in mind. To quote the overworked examples, different answers were given if he wanted to travel on the railway, see a horror film without adult accompaniment, drive a motor car or fly an aeroplane, drink intoxicating liquor in a public place or marry without parental approval. Another complaint from the same source was that the community in general tended to delay recognition and insist on treating the older adolescent as a child when he had ceased to be one. During the last decade there have been changes which have gone some way to meet both these complaints. The point about the new legislation is not that it changes social attitudes (though it may contribute to this), not even that it clears up all the ambiguities in the social position of the teenager, but that it recognizes a social change which has taken place. This was the conclusion of the Latey Committee[12] whose recommendations lie behind the new legislation. They found that young people of seventeen and onwards were thinking of themselves as adults and increasingly being regarded as such by other older adults.

What are the implications here for Youth Service? Simply that if youngsters of 18 see themselves as adults and are encouraged in this by the community, they will be less likely to join organizations which include the under 16s. Of course, the question arises whether Youth Service should exist at all for young adults: or to put the issue more accurately—since 'Youth Service' may be the wrong title for this age group now, is there a need for a leisure time provision for the older teenagers? Can they not be left to make their own arrangements helped by the commercial providers and able anyway to join in adult facilities of all kinds including the opportunities in further education? There are after all natural reasons why many young people leave youth organizations—pairing off in courting couples, earlier marriages and demands of work, training and service in the community.

Such evidence as we have suggests that there are many youngsters over 18 in our society (some would say up to 25) who need provision for their leisure time activities if they are to enjoy that leisure and continue their social and personal education. Bernard Davies who has been among the sternest critics of the existing service, is sure that the community must organize a service for the older teenagers. '. . . it does seem to me inconceivable that the Youth Service should simply turn its back on this social group of the late teenager since so many within it do seem completely unserved in a way which is genuinely personal and without ulterior motive.'[13] This view is supported by the experiences of 'detached workers amongst the unattached'. During the last decade there have been a few experimental ventures like the National Association of Youth Clubs' project reported on by Mary Morse and the Y.W.C.A. Paddington Coffee Bar Experiment.[14] Partly as a consequence of these pioneering efforts there are now a few established workers of this kind in the field. All their reports agree that there are many youngsters in our society over 17 of both sexes who need some help, not at present forthcoming, to get more out of life and establish themselves in the adult world. They are often bored, lack the social confidence to move out of their immediate neighbourhood for entertainment, find it difficult to make stable relationships, are vocationally uncertain, often unhappy and sometimes delinquent. Goestchius and Tash called them 'the can't copes'. Whilst we are not suggesting that the Service should exist only for the sake of these socially needy youngsters, their presence in the country belies the belief that Youth Service could stop at about 16. A general conviction among those who have pondered the issue is that many young people of 17 and over have needs which they share with older members of the community but many, perhaps the majority, have needs peculiar to their age and social position; and these needs are recognizably different from the needs of children and younger teenagers. Equally widespread is the view that these distinctive needs are not commonly met in existing youth organizations.

In the earlier part of this chapter we looked at what we called the 'juvenile image' and gave the causes arising from the organization of Youth Service itself and from changes in our society. But a more powerful cause arises from the atmosphere of particular clubs and centres and groups. These are often paternalistic and sometimes authoritarian. They are geared to the needs of youngsters in their mid-teens rather than the late-teens. This is supported by one or two enquiries among young people who had experience in youth organizations. 'There was a strong feeling that there was not enough opportunity for freedom of expression, independent action and programme planning by members themselves.'

Workers in the field have every right to expect that they should be supported by a national policy which has been carefully thought through and corresponds to the needs of young people today. This probably means that the present age span from 14 to 21 is too broad since the needs of youngsters at the higher end are not the same as those at the lower end: the present situation calls for a 'junior' and a 'senior' section though these would not be the best titles. Youth workers have also the right to expect that a relevant national policy will be supported and implemented by local authorities; they should not be frustrated by an unreasonable degree of apathy in their own area. In the light of the present discussion they should have an Education Committee which appreciates the different approaches which can be made to the late teenagers.

But the commonest reason for the failure to serve the 17s and upwards is the atmosphere and approaches of the local youth group and the behaviour of the worker. Improvements here offer the best chance of hopeful change.

The fault may lie in the personality and attitudes of the youth worker. In the worst cases, he may be authoritarian with a need to dominate others: he does not see the members as other than children dependent on him for support, discipline and guidance. The character trait will affect his style of performance and his relationships with young people. There is still at least one club where the leader blows a whistle to command silence! In less extreme cases, the leader may be unwilling to accept the ideas of young people and concede them genuine self determination, because he fears the consequences of a loss of control: perhaps he feels under threat from his superiors in the organization who would regard any such development with disapproval: or he himself feels happier if the enterprise is tidy with clear rules and organized activities and visible successes in competitive triumphs.

Like other community workers, youth workers need on-going training which will help them to look objectively at themselves and what they are doing.[15] This is best achieved by the supervision which is described elsewhere in this book. By this arrangement, the youth worker discusses with a 'tutor' his own account of what he saw and what he did in the youth group. In this way, since the 'tutor' acts as a sounding board, he is encouraged to reflect upon and assess his own performance. There is however no immediate prospect of all the operatives in the service receiving supervisory help; we are not yet within sight of providing this for full-time leaders. Meanwhile, in a growing number of areas, there are further training courses whose main intention is to expose the practising youth worker to his own weaknesses, to increase self-awareness and sensitivity rather than merely to give information or teach activity skills. These courses are based on the simple proposition that in the end all training in social work skills is self-training. Only the most complacent will avoid further training. The alarming truth about our faults as community workers is that we are unconscious of them. Even the authoritarian leader does not see himself as such.

A growing sensitivity to the needs of young people can take the youth worker a long way but not all the way. The recognition has to be expressed in the structure, policy and programme of the organization. There are, for example, youth clubs where there are special privileges, opportunities and activities for those over 16 or 17 or 18. In some places, there is a separate senior members' night. But elsewhere this simple recognition is not accorded and nineteen year olds share the same programme with thirteen year olds and compete with them for facilities and equipment. This is not usually part of a conscious policy to create community feeling by mixing youngsters of different ages: more frequently it is associated with leadership which is either not aware of the situation, or, being aware, is too lazy or apathetic or dispirited to adjust the programme. This negativism is usually found among youth workers who seek to be 'lone wolves', not learning or caring about what others are doing, running a club rather than seeking to make a small contribution to the social education of a new generation, happily rotating in the narrow confines of their own limited experience. The remedy is not far to seek since there can be few areas of the country where possibilities do not exist for youth workers to meet to compare notes, share experiences and exchange ideas.

Nor can the worker on the shop floor be absolved from a responsibility to affect policy in his local government authority. He may be a member of the local Youth Committee; he may serve on any one of half a dozen local committees which can affect policy in his area, like the local S.C.N.V.Y.O. or an area denominational committee or the regional committee of a national voluntary organization. Even when this is not the case he can still have opportunities of influencing local youth policy since in a democracy committees are expected to take account of public opinion. Youth Service in most areas is a relatively close-knit community of interested people who see each other regularly; most club leaders for example know their local authority Youth Officer personally.

Above some other services, Youth Service offers opportunities to shop floor workers to influence policy and that is why a general exploration like this is relevant for them. In the present discussion, it is possible that an adult and sophisticated approach to the late teenagers—related to but distinct from the rest of the provision—may encounter opposition. The new forms will be less administratively tidy since they will be client-centred, not based on buildings or membership; will contain more elements of self-determination by young people and will be less under adult control and less fashioned by adult purposiveness; will raise emotional issues such as whether young adults over 18 should not have intoxicating drink in their meeting places; will be seen to be present in many places in the community (not only in official headquarters) like industry and commercial centres of entertainment (a point to which we return later). For these and other reasons there may well be strong opposition to the new approaches from administrators in the education service especially if those administrators are tinged with bureaucracy.

Youth workers may find that only with a struggle will they encourage a 'young adult' service for the 17s and over. They should have the courage to act upon their convictions.

LIMITED APPEAL FOR GIRLS

Baden-Powell wrote *Scouting for Boys* in 1907. It has often been pointed out that he was surprised and overwhelmed by the response; in its beginnings, the Scout movement is a fine example of the spontaneous upsurge of enthusiasm when the contemporary needs of the young are catered for. What is not widely appreciated is that the response from the girls—leading eventually to the Girl Guide movement—was even more unexpected; the many girls who wanted to join in the new game were in fact a source of embarrassment to the founders.

As early as 1909, at the Crystal Palace Rally, Baden-Powell was confronted by a band of Girl Scouts. This development threatened the movement with disrepute since many older people considered scouting unsuitable for girls. There is a comic element in the early attempts to accommodate girls in the movement. They had to be recognized since they existed. But what were they to be called? 'Girl Guides' was an early choice for the senior section but 'Rosebuds' was the first suggestion for those who are now called 'Brownies'. How were the two programmes for boys and girls to be related? What about the uniform? These were vexed questions at the time. The whole incident, and the fact that it never occurred to Baden-Powell to plan for girls, is typical of the history of youth movements in this country. Generally they are founded for boys and the girls are allowed to join in or are thought of afterwards. The Y.M.C.A. was established in 1844, the Y.W.C.A. in 1855; the Boys' Brigade in 1883, the Girls' Life Brigade in 1902. The Federation of London Working Boys' Clubs was formed in 1888; girls' clubs first began to be organized nationally in 1895.

The primacy of boys in youth service is partly explained by general social and cultural factors prevailing at the time. These youth movements arose in a male-dominated society where men wielded the power and controlled the resources. Perhaps it was tacitly understood that in an industrial society, the home continued to be a bigger influence in the socialization of girls; they can continue to learn in the family how to play their major social roles of wife and mother but boys have to look beyond the home for training for the male role as an industrial worker. Youth service was more instant and lavish in its provision for boys since they were seen to be in greater need.

How do these pointers from the past help us to understand the provision for girls in the Youth Service today and their response to the provision? There are of course famous and well-established organizations catering for girls only, such as the Girl Guides. But across the whole spectrum of the service, there are far fewer girls in the membership of youth groups than boys; they join later and leave earlier. The current statistics (1969) for one large city, Birmingham, can be taken as typical. There are 13,741 males between 14 and 20 in the membership of youth organizations, but only 7,990 girls. If attention is concentrated on the 17 to 20 age group, the disparity is more striking—6,203 males and 2,471 females.

Again, as in the past, there are reasons outside the scope and control of Youth Service, in our society as a whole, which partly explain this relative lack of feminine response. One is that there is not an equal number of boys and girls available as recruits; there are not enough girls to balance the sexes. One aspect of the subject is demographic. In most societies, including Britain until recent times, more boys are born than girls but since, in the past it has been more dangerous to be born male than female, the balance was restored by about the age of ten. But with the improvement in medical knowledge and care, more juvenile males survive in a country like Britain. It has been estimated, for example, that by 1983 the number of men of working age in Britain will exceed the number of women of working age by one million and a half. There is also a social and cultural aspect of the situation. Girls are still expected in many places to share more household duties than boys, like shopping, baby-sitting, washing and ironing. In working class households of Liverpool it is reported that women would be shocked and horrified if male members of the family undertook 'women's work' in the home. Once inside a youth organization, girls are less likely to be appointed to its committees or its offices, and, on the whole, members of organizations who are appointed to executive positions retain their association longer since presumably they gain more significance and emotional income from office-bearing. This again reflects what is happening in society at large. Most committees have a predominance of male members; in many respects ours is still a male-dominated society where power, influence and leadership are found more commonly in the hands of men and women are expected to play a subservient role. 'Men do not always realize how much courage it still needs for even a practised woman member of a committee to "set herself up as an authority". For girls who are seldom in a position of authority at home or work, the effort is still greater.'[16]

Nor can the subject of girls in youth organizations be viewed separately from a larger debate which is going on in Britain about the present and future social role of women and the relationship of the sexes. On the one hand are those who emphasize aspects of change. The male and female roles are less sharply defined and contrasted, witness the current confusion in the role symbols of dress and hair styles among the young. Women for a variety of reasons—the pill, better education, going out to work—are, on this view, giving up their massive pre-occupation with personal relationships; they are beginning to be interested in 'things'; they have wider interests; they are not content any longer to find their total fulfilment in wifehood and motherhood. If this is true it has big implications for the educational programmes of youth groups. But there are those who do not agree. They question how far the social role of woman can ever be separated from her biological role as wife and mother; they expect women to go on looking towards these two roles for their major social significance. If that is true then organizers of youth groups must expect girls to come 'looking for a boy'.

But the issue is not settled yet. And Youth Service cannot be expected to know the answer; nor can it be a major agent of social change; it can only reflect the social situation as it exists and that at the moment is not known. If mixed youth groups concentrated on providing for the 'new twentieth century woman' they might well find themselves even more out of touch with their clientele. On the other hand, if they conclude that most girls are pre-occupied with the desire to be wives and mothers, they may find the service is out of date. To some extent the dilemma 'what to do with the girls in a mixed youth club' mirrors the ambiguity of women's role in contemporary society.

On the whole however, the balance of opinion would be in favour of the view that girls focus their attention on their family role. Margaret Mead[17] examined a number of primitive societies in the South Seas to discover which sex distinctions were biologically determined and which came from the prevailing culture. Many of her findings upset our conventional expectations. She discovered, for example, that among the Tchambuli, the men wear false curls and ornaments, paint and arrange theatricals while the women are unadorned, shave their heads and attend to the business affairs of the community. Yet certain invariable sex traits were found throughout these different societies, one being the masculine emphasis upon active achievement and the feminine emphasis upon the great passive achievement of bearing children. Contemporary women writers pleading for a larger recognition of girls' interests in youth groups, whilst arguing that girls have wider interests than is usually supposed, admit that their basic search in the group is for a young man who will fall in love with them.

> It is important to note that the girl's sphere of interest has widened enormously over the past few years. Rifle-shooting, pot-holing, canoeing, pottery, drama, art, archery and committee work are some of the activities she shares today with boys . . . but there is still the need for her to develop as a woman—as a

budgetter, buyer, dressmaker, cook, interior dectorator, nurse, hostess, voter, partner and mother.

All activities concerned with home-making have an appeal for most girls. . . .[18] If that is the case, the question arises whether a youth organization is likely to prove the best agent of socialization for the majority of girls. Clearly the family of origin still has a big part to play. It has been pointed out by Dr Cyril Smith that teenage pop culture may be a greater socializing force for girls than boys since much of it is concerned with love and marriage. If girls see the club as primarily a point of romantic social contact, a hunting ground for the likely male partner, are they likely to become involved in the youth organization with its demand for loyalty, the offer of activities, and different types of relationships including the 'non-sexual'? Advocates of youth movements say that it is just because of a girl's major pre-occupation that she may need a mixed group to belong to; here her interests can be widened; she can learn to share many activities with boys and develop her personality to become more discriminating in her choices and make a better life partner with a brighter chance of an enduring marriage. The development of many girls cannot simply be left to the other agencies of socialization like formal education, the home and commercial entertainment because there are still so many socially needy girls left when these agencies have done their work.

This brings us to the final and most practical point. Among those who have thought long and carefully on the subject there is a consensus of opinion which may be expressed as follows:
Mixed youth groups probably have much to offer to a majority of adolescent girls in our society. But not as those youth groups are most frequently organized today. They are intended, planned, and continued for boys and the girls can tag along if they wish. As one observer puts it, 'The boys have the clubs; the girls have the powder room.'

Once again the major hope of improvement lies—not with pronouncements from the Department of Education and Science or from changes in local authority policy—but with raising the performance of the local youth group. The leader occupies a key position in these possibilities though clearly he must gain the support for a genuinely mixed youth group policy and programme from his helpers and the management committee.

The underlying and recurrent weakness of the mixed youth group, from the girl's point of view, is that the enterprise has not been thought through, the project is not related to a philosophy of mixed youth work; in other words it has been planned, albeit unconsciously, with boys in mind. This is to put the matter in general terms but there are specific aspects of the situation.

There is first the stark fact that most mixed youth groups have a male leader; some do not even count a woman helper among the staff. Women writers on this subject agree that the male leader can encourage girls in what they often lack—efficiency, skill and self-confidence; but they are equally emphatic that the biological difference makes it impossible even for the most perceptive male leader to understand the problems of adolescent girls. Positively, he will have an inevitable disposition to interpret members' needs in the light of his own male experience; for example, he is likely to be more encouraging to activities which show a return for money in competitive results or raising levels of skill; he is likely to be less sympathetic to 'just having fun', gossiping and the development of social relationships. Dr Macalister Brew used to say that those who fail with girls are those who try to lead them either as if they are boys or as if it is a pity they are not boys, or as if they can be boys if they try hard enough. Although women leaders may perform in this way too, clearly males are more disposed to the interpretation. Gaining recognition of girls in the Youth Service begins at the simple and obvious place of increasing and improving the female leadership of the local unit.

Related to the previous paragraph is a second feature. Only rarely do we find a mixed youth group where the psychology of the adolescent girl is understood as well as that of the adolescent boy. Again, women writers on the subject stress the girl's need to prove an attractive woman. Other aspects of understanding the girl spring from this main definition. She is interested in people rather than things; wants to be treated as a young adult at an earlier age than the boy; is more acutely aware of the conventions attaching to a social behaviour. Girls we are told, respond to a service where they find personal encouragement, are helped to understand themselves and can discuss their personal problems at a time of rapid social change. In areas of experience which they share with boys, like work, their needs are different; boys will probably be interested in promotion prospects but girls concentrate more on the personal relationships at work. Not that these writers see the club as only supplying what the girls think they want; the club can provide an educational approach which may correct a 'too feminine' approach to life, widening girls' interests in the world outside the home and saving them from a compulsive and exclusive concern with their role as wife and mother.

If the policy of mixed youth work has been thought through at the local level and there is appropriate adult help for girls as well as boys, and if the whole enterprise is permeated by an understanding of the needs of girls, then all this will find expression in the programme of the group, in the activities and interests which are encouraged and organized.

There are, of course, appropriate single-sexed activities for girls in a mixed unit, and though youth workers often complain that 'they do not know what to do with the girls', on enquiry it is often found that they have shown little imagination or patience, have not related the education and pastoral offers to the needs of girls, or have expected the girls to be attracted by the same competitive opportunities that appeal to boys. The Duke of Edinburgh's Award Scheme for girls, for example, under the section 'Design for Living' offers possibilities such as 'What to wear and when to wear it', 'Courtesy and Customs', 'Acquiring your home', 'Entertaining' and 'The Art of Make-up and Hairstyles'. A course on homemaking can be comprehensive and is a liberal education in itself. Other possibilities ought to recognize the changing role of women in society, that many girls may not be content to be completely absorbed by love, courtship and marriage; some of them at least will respond to interests and activities not necessarily connected with their sex role. But the justification for mixed groups is that it is important for young people of both sexes to do many things together. Segregation of the sexes in education is potentially dangerous. Adolescent youths and girls need each other—to learn about the opposite sex, to become whole human beings, to have more fun, to mature socially and emotionally, to learn how to discriminate among the bewildering choices which are offered to them in a modern society. The mixed activities should be carefully thought through in the light of these primary goals. Some pursuits are clearly single-sexed—boxing for boys, the make-up group still (one hopes) for girls. A few activities which were unambiguously single-sexed a few years ago, like cooking, are happily used by both sexes now. But there are activities—drama is a good example—which satisfy the male's clamant need for achievement, the female's clamant need for self-expression and help male and female to profit by co-operation with the opposite sex.

The place of the girls in the mixed youth organization tests the sensitivity and the patience of the youth worker and measures his (or her) willingness to seek outside help and ideas and to learn from what others are doing. To plead that the needs of girls should receive due recognition is only a special aspect of the plea that Youth Service should be client-centred, existing primarily for the benefit of the young people.

MORE THAN BUILDINGS AND ORGANIZATIONS

Two education officers meet over coffee at an annual conference. A. asks B.: 'And what is your youth work like?' The answer could well be couched in terms of the new youth centres opened or planned: the number of full-time workers involved; the weekly attendance at statutory clubs and the strength of the voluntary organizations; the drama festival and public-speaking competition. In other words, the education officer is equating 'youth work' with 'Youth Service': it is something that takes place in a building and is associated with membership organizations. This is the point of view which is proving today to be limiting and inadequate.

The education officer makes a common error. There is a widespread unexamined assumption that there are only a few ways of doing youth work—clubs, uniformed organizations and special activity groups. In some quarters indeed 'Youth work equals clubs'. The Albemarle Report, for example, to repeat a point made in the last section, planned an expansion of the Service but it was an expansion which was almost exclusively concerned with a building programme and the recruitment of more members to existing organizations. '. . . the recommendations of the Albemarle Committee were extensively based on the knowledge and experience of youth organizations as they existed in the late 1950s; a glance at the organizations which submitted evidence will tend to confirm this. It is, therefore, hardly surprising if the Youth Service has grown up against this background and has, in the process, greatly strengthened what we may now call the "orthodox" youth club provision.'[19] One of the few books to be devoted to the history of Youth Service,[20] does not envisage any development of the work outside organizations.

The limited outlook is understandable and indeed almost inevitable in view of the history of youth work in this country. Early founders of youth movements saw themselves as protecting young people against the evils and neglect of their society: they sought to inhabit an island of light in a sea of darkness: separate organizations were unavoidable. 'All education may well mean some separation of the young person from his origins, but the values implicit in early youth work were in direct opposition to the background of young people whom it sought to serve. It was assumed from the start that the ultimate ideal could be attained only if young people were taken almost completely out of the values and habits of the world of their parents and launched into a world which the providers had defined as more valuable.'[21]

This way of thinking of the work has not fundamentally changed in the twentieth century (when much else has changed in Youth Service) and has become a stereotyped approach. That a major change will come easily is an unrealistic expectation. The two partners—statutory and voluntary—combine in preferring a system where heads can be counted, where there are tangible tests of success and which is administratively tidy. Those demands are better met by a provision which is usually limited to buildings and organizations with a definite membership. As in most other human activities, the officials begin to have a vested interest—emotional certainly, economic perhaps—in the associations with which they are involved. Its success is their success—and they require visible measurements of success. To have a client-centred Youth Service—to take it to young people wherever they are—to be content that young people should be served and not necessarily counted—that requires constant decisions of courage and unselfishness. Recently in Britain, consternation and anxiety were aroused by rumours that the new government report on Youth Service would see an end of clubs and centres; assurance had to be given that there was an inevitable continuity in the work; fresh approaches might be made but the old approaches could not be immediately abandoned. Not all the concern expressed at this time was on behalf of the young people.

What we are here pleading for is that within the framework of the general purpose we have previously defined, 'youth work' should be seen to be able to take many forms and appear in many places; that in particular, its methods of informal education have a wider usefulness than their employment in conventional youth organizations.

There is less excuse today for the failure to take this more generous and flexible view if only because there are already many examples of youth work taking place in 'unorthodox' settings and various reports which have commented favourably on this development.

As to the first, we have elsewhere described in detail the development of 'youth work in the schools' in the decade after Albemarle. J. M. Hogan, one of the most enthusiastic advocates of this approach, found it necessary to say: 'Many will disagree with me about the sweeping conclusion to which I have come, i.e. that there is nothing which has been stated about the aims of Youth Service in the past that cannot and indeed ought not, to be assumed as a major responsibility of a secondary school.'[22] If it is not too prejudiced an interpretation, the Newsom Report *(Half our Future)* can be seen as a tribute to Youth Service since the suggestion is there made to carry its methods into the secondary school. 'These girls and boys must somehow be made much more active partners in their own education.' Colleges of education, as we have seen, were encouraged to offer optional courses to students in teacher training. Research into the results of those courses establishes that though few of those students subsequently become full-time leaders (as the Albemarle Report expected) yet a strong impression remains (as we have seen) that they are 'better teachers': their skill in less obviously didactic approaches is enhanced.

It is not only the schools however which have become new centres for youth work. The National Association of Boys' Clubs have specialized in running short residential courses of adjustment to industry. Warwickshire is one authority which has devoted special attention to the same method. And for several years the Sheffield diocese has had a centre at Castleton used for a like purpose. Youth work methods have also been found to be appropriate for remand homes, approved schools, detention centres and Borstal institutions. There is at least one course for residential child care officers which offers to students the possibility of youth work experience.

Outside institutions, there are far more examples of 'experimental' work in the last ten years than is usually realized: the file on the subject compiled by the Information Centre reveals a rich variety.

Nor has this wider interpretation of youth work been confined to actual pieces of work: there are a growing number of cases where the thinking of organizers and providers has broken loose from the narrow confines of clubs, brigades, etc. The Derbyshire Report, already quoted, was so emphatic in its emphasis upon the younger end being catered for by school, and the older end being cared for by adult organizations, that it hastily reassured its readers that it still saw a place for the conventional youth club.

There remain new territories for youth work though they may only be entered by invitation and as an aspect of co-operation: one is industry, the other is the realm of commercial provision of entertainment. The writer recalls two recent instructive experiences. The first was a day when in a large city, he visited three huge industrial undertakings to talk with the personnel officers responsible for the welfare and, to some extent, the social and recreational opportunities of young employees. They were men of immense goodwill and with considerable resources at their command. Yet one or two things were fairly obvious. They could have profited by sharing the experiences of youth workers —their understanding of adolescence and their grasp of helpful techniques. Equally many Youth Service officials and workers would have benefited from sharing the personnel officers' expert knowledge of young people at work. Yet so far as one could see there had been no contact between the two types of education/social workers charged with care of the young. The second occasion was a visit in a Northern city to a series of licensed discotheques organized for young people. These proved to be in the hands of surprisingly young managers who had received scant training for their duties. In conversation they recalled the times when youngsters had come to them with personal problems for help and advice: but often they had been at a loss to help, often not even knowing the name of the right social agency for referral. Yet nobody in the city was offering youth work training for managers of licensed discotheques!

If Youth Service is to rise to the level of its present opportunities, it will need to move out of its buildings and organizations, whilst continuing to maintain what is already established there. Youth work should be seen as the type of relationship across the generations which we have described in an earlier section: it will take many forms only some of which will be clubs and companies and troops: it will be found in many places, not only in buildings set aside for the purpose.

The new definition has strong implications for the youth worker. It challenges his insularity, and rebukes the over-commitment to one method, or organization, or even unit, which is a form of tribe loyalty. It encourages us to welcome as colleagues many people whose work brings them into a responsible relationship with young people but who would not at present everywhere be counted as part of the Youth Service. It invites us to encourage new forms of endeavour which seek to meet young people's needs for social education, for fun, interests, counselling and participation. In particular, it encourages a wider interpretation of the role of the professional full-time youth

F

worker. He should see himself committed to the young people of a neighbourhood, not just to those who come to a club or a centre. And if his employers have narrower expectations, and if his conditions of work do not permit of a wider constituency, he should have the courage courteously to argue for a more magnanimous interpretation. And if in the end he decides to serve young people outside youth organizations (say as adviser about young industrial workers, as happened to one recently) none of us—least of all himself—should think that 'he has left Youth Service'.

We have been arguing in this chapter that we should learn in our thinking and practice not to divide young people into those within youth organizations and those outside: nor must we by our efforts segregate young people from other age groups in the community. But that is the argument of a later chapter.

INSULATION WITHOUT ISOLATION

The section heading is adapted from a report published in 1945.[28] Commending the value of youth groups being accommodated in buildings used for all age groups it says: 'The principle should be insulation within the same whole rather than any isolation or segregation from the whole.'

It is a neat phrase and for a time became a fashionable quotation until it passed into a tiresome cliché. Yet the phrase briefly expresses a continuing ideal for Youth Service, namely that adolescents shall be understood as passing through a distinctive stage of human development, yet not so as to think of them as being basically different from other members of the community. Hence youth organizations should not separate them from the rest of the community but help them to live and find their place in it: whilst at the same time recognizing that they will have some needs which are not shared by all the other members of the community. Most people are looking for acceptance and security and significance but older people are not usually concerned with problems of personal identity, choosing a job and a life partner.

Youth work then is judged to be effective when it offers insulation without isolation. Behind this lie more general issues of the understanding of young people in a country like ours. They can best be described by the rejection of two common phrases which depict opposing attitudes.

'The duty of an adolescent,' it has been said, 'is to stop being one.' At worst this sentence suggests that adolescence is a sickness from which we should recover. At best, it sees adolescence as an experience which has value mainly as preparing for what comes after: not as a stage to be enjoyed now for its own sake: at best a blossom to give way to the fruit, and a blossom in whose beauty we should not delight if no fruit follows.

But others say, in excusing even the heartless and selfish behaviour of some adolescents, 'Let them alone: you are only young once', as though the kind of adults they will become bears little relation to the kind of young people they are; as though there is no unity in human experience and one phase of development can be separated from another.

'Insulation without isolation' can be interpreted to mean a recognition of adolescence both as a stage of development in its own right, to be enjoyed as such, and yet also a preparation for what comes after. Writers on the psychology of adolescence vary according to whether they stress the youngster's affinity with people of any age in the community, or whether they stress that they see him primarily as on a journey which is justified by the destination of adulthood.

For Freudians, adolescence is the dramatic prelude to adulthood, to be understood as a developmental task. The individual finds himself challenged by adult sexuality and by a resurgence of emotional difficulties unresolved in earlier years. If the challenge of these conflicts is accepted, the individual can move on to stable adulthood: if they are not accepted, the earlier conflicts are driven more deeply into the personality.

To the youth workers, these may seem highly theoretical matters. But the issue has practical implications. Reflecting upon our work, we may consider that we have isolated adolescence from the rest of the member's experience and the adolescent from his community: or we may judge that we have not taken sufficient account of the needs of the adolescent because he is at a particular stage of the human journey.

On the whole, the commoner criticism in recent years has been an accusation that Youth Service tends to segregate teenagers from the rest of the community, that in fact, it isolates without insulating. The issue is not always understood. One of the most quoted statements of aims came from the pen of Sir John Maude. 'To offer individual young people in their leisure time opportunities of various kinds,

69

complementary to those of home, formal education and work, to discover and develop their personal resources of body, mind and spirit and thus to better equip themselves to live the life of mature, creative and responsible members of a free society.' Here the complementary aims of personal development and community involvement are nicely balanced. But in practice—in the policy of an area or the habits of a particular unit—it is not unusual to find one stressed to the neglect of the other.

Some of the criticism about segregation is directed against the notion of having a Youth Service at all. Why should there be separate leisure time provision for teenagers? Those under 17 should find what they want in the schools; those over 17 can join adult organizations. Is there any place for a Youth Service when there are the Youth Employment Service, Further Education, clubs of many kinds and a vast range of commercial provision? May it not even do harm in concentrating public attention on 'youth', encouraging a 'youth cult' and 'teenage culture', make the youngsters feel self-conscious, contribute to the conviction that 'teenagers' are a special species and create a 'youth problem' by acting as if there were one?

Whether justly or not, this view has come to be associated with Dr F. Musgrove, among others. 'The Albemarle Report on the Youth Service in England and Wales is one of the most disastrous social documents to appear in this country this century. It widens the fissure in English society which divides the generations and, no doubt with the best intentions in the world, belittles and humiliates the young. It advocates that there be established a separate, segregated, adolescent world (for young people between 14 and 20) with specially trained (and paid) representatives of adult society to supervise and oversee it. . . . There is, throughout the Report, no conception of introducing young people into adult institutions, even as junior members.'[24] It is true, of course, as we have already observed, that the Albemarle Report planned an expansion of youth work largely within youth organizations and gave little attention to developments in the community as a whole.

Most critics, however, would not accuse Youth Service *per se* of segregating young people from the rest of the community. They consider that there is still a need to provide for the social development of many young people away from home, school, further education and commercial provision. And this service needs to be identified for administrative purposes or it may well fail to command the support it needs. To leave many young people to all-age or adult provision in our society is to fail at present to recognize their special needs: they are 'adults' (as we have argued elsewhere) but they are 'young adults' and the adjective can prove as important as the noun. But these second critics agree that often Youth Service is in fact operating in isolation. At worst, it is concerned with buildings and organizations: at best it is dedicated to the individual's development but does not see him as a member of a wider community than the club or centre.

This brings us once again to the local youth unit. Sometimes one suspects that dedicated and well-intentioned leaders are simply working with a false picture of what they are trying to do. They see the club or centre, company or troop, as a segment cut out of a community. The insularity and even the possessiveness of some youth workers has often been commented upon: in the worst cases they are afraid 'to lose their young people' to other forms of community work.

Pressures for a community-related Youth Service come from different quarters. Some approach it from the angle of the needs of young people—they cannot be served or understood as isolated individuals but as people involved with the community: others approach it from the standpoint of the needs of the community which requires responsible and caring citizens. What will happen, for example, unless another army of voluntary social workers is forthcoming from the new generation? Some support the view because in an old-fashioned way, they think it is the duty of youth organizations to teach young people to conform to the existing values of the social order. They receive support from all those, including some government officials, who see Youth Service as having mainly a socializing function. Others see possibilities for a more critical and active involvement of young people in their community: the young have a right to change society as well as accept it. Others—among them the Eppels and Musgrove—approach the subject from their research findings which show that the young are not as alienated from the adult community as is often supposed. Musgrove, in his sample, discovered that it was commoner for adults to reject teenagers than vice versa. Yet others emphasize the country's need for the encouragement of community feeling. They may do this as part of a social philosophy, or, as the officers of the National Federation of Community Association, from their experience of working in all-age community organizations. The Peckham Health

Centre experiment is quoted with approval since it made provision for all the family in one building.

What practical measures can encourage a Youth Service which insulates without isolating and does not in fact encourage the segregation of young people from their community?

Once again we begin at the point of a national policy to be supported by local authorities.

1 We need a broad definition of youth work as something which takes place not merely in organizations and buildings set aside for the purpose but in all those places where younger and older people are brought together. Youth officers could, we repeat, often be accepted as colleagues by personnel officers in industry and by managers of dance halls, skating rinks and licensed discotheques.

2 This may well imply more consultation between different government departments and local authority sections who have different responsibilities for young people.

3 Leisure time provision for young people can be encouraged in many more places than youth centres or youth groups, and particularly in places where other age groups are catered for.

4 Political education should not be automatically omitted from the programme of youth organizations for though party conflict should be excluded, many issues today are controversial and young people should be actively involved if they are to take their proper place in a democracy.

Whilst we may look forward to this broadening and expansion of youth work in the community, yet it is in the youth organizations themselves that the next steps can be taken. Any youth worker for whom the 'insulation-isolation' issue is relevant, might ponder the following considerations.

1 What is the real aim of our work? Are we seeking better club members or young people who can take their place happily, confidently, responsibly in the community as husbands or wives, fathers or mothers and citizens?

2 How do we 'see' the young person who uses our facilities? As a 'club member' or as a young person who has a life outside the club—at home, work, in leisure and friendship groups, street, neighbourhood?

3 How far does our understanding of him recognize that he needs 'fun now and preparation for the next stage of his growth'?

4 What opportunities are provided for the young person to accept responsibility, to make decisions, to affect policy and to bear the consequences of his choices?

5 How many links are built between the club and the community? Do notices on the board announce what is happening outside or are they only about club events and personalities? Does the programme bring interesting visitors into the club to talk about and demonstrate their jobs and concerns? How much informal conversation is concerned with what is happening outside the club? How many visits are arranged to places of interest? Are there opportunities for the young people to give voluntary service—jobs not chosen for them by older people, but chosen by the young people themselves after considering the needs of their neighbourhood?

A youth organization should, so to speak, be on the highway, not tucked away from it.

RAISING WORKERS' SKILLS

It will by now be clear to the reader that there are one or two recurring themes in the present work. Perhaps the most persistent is the conviction that the best hope of improving the Service is in an increase in the skill of the shop floor workers whether part-time or professional: even a slight all-round improvement here would have major consequences for a new generation, far more determinative than the announcement of a new government policy. One does not under-rate the value of policy, still less the value of suitable premises and adequate equipment, but when one looks at particular pieces of work there is an undeniable factor—the success or failure of the enterprise relates closely to the quality of the adults involved in the work.

There are in Britain plenty of salutary examples where two similar pieces of youth work exist in the same town or suburb. So far as one can see the circumstances of both are much the same. They recruit members from the same social class. Their premises and equipment are comparable. Yet with like opportunities, very different results are achieved—and here there is no implied reference to triumphs in competitions or festivals. The difference exists mostly in a contrasted atmosphere. In the first, one feels that a high value is placed on anybody who enters the doors, not because of something he may become—a Christian, say, or a late entrant for 'A' levels through the encouragement he receives in the club—but because of what he is now, simply

73

a human being. And this high evaluation is expressed in a score of ways, not all of them written. (If it did not sound so banal, one might say, 'Love will find a way.') It expresses itself in the notices on the board, in the way the coffee is handed over the counter, in the tone and bearing of workers and members. In the other place, one feels that people do not care. And certainly, indifference will find a way of expressing itself. Nobody bothers, for example—and this is a most conspicuous mark of indifference—to communicate, that is to tell other people what they need to know, at the right time and in a form that they can understand. Here also one finds that decisions may be taken without any genuine attempt to discover the desires and feelings of those who will be affected. Again, the first situation is an exciting place. New things are happening all the time. No sooner have they finished the Christmas concert for the old-age pensioners, than they are beginning to talk, *inter alia*, about an Easter visit to Coventry Cathedral: and already there is a notice on the board about a club holiday in the Black Forest during August. The menu, so to speak, includes a long list of items: in fact, one is confronted by many choices, not a set meal for every customer. By contrast, the second situation is characterized by dullness and staleness: it is the restricted mixture as before: nothing new ever seems to happen.

One does not wish to be more specific in identifying the locations of these strange contrasts: it is certainly not the way to make friends or influence people. But the point to be made here is a fairly obvious one. The major factor in success or failure as defined above is the quality and outlook and skill of the adults concerned with the work: later, an attempt is made to describe the relevant qualities in more detail.

It is not surprising, then, that in the decade after Albemarle 'leadership', both professional and part-time, was a major pre-occupation in Youth Service. As we have seen, there were big changes in the curriculum and intention of training courses for full-time operatives. Two reports on training part-time workers[25] were issued by the Department of Education and Science. Several books were devoted to the subject. It was fortunate that Dr T. R. Batten was involved in Youth Service during this period: he brought a special contribution from his long experiences of training social workers for developing countries: for the most part, his stress on non-directive approaches were taken up enthusiastically by the 'trainers' in Youth Service.

The following list is an attempted summary of the emphasis in the thinking about 'Youth Leadership' which claimed attention during the period under review.

a It is a highly skilled job, not a piece of casual labour. And the heart of the skill is 'social group method'. (In the case of the full-time operatives, this was not unconnected with the desire to give prestige to a professional role.) Primarily the youth worker is not a community organizer concerned with the general public nor a caseworker usually involved with one other person in an interview situation. He is concerned to help a group of young people to develop their own resources; to grow out of their need of him; to function in such a way that every single member of the group can profit by the presence of every other member. Hence the stress in 'social group method', not merely on correct techniques, but on democratic philosophy and intention. In Youth Service circles, to call a worker 'authoritarian' has become the equivalent of swearing at him. Though indeed the whole discussion has been widely misunderstood. 'Democratic' has been taken to mean 'passive': the 'facilitator' has not been carefully distinguished from the 'spectator'. Similarly, 'authoritarian' has been confused with 'having proper authority'. The first, in the Adorno sense, refers to the man who actually enjoys pushing others around, who has a psychological need to dominate. The second refers to what is inseparable from the exercise of leadership. We can all think of youth group situations where the passive leader, lacking proper authority, would not survive for a single night.

b In former days, the focus of attention was on the youth worker's ability to institute and sustain activities. This is not suddenly seen to be without any value: the techniques of informal education are an essential part of the youth worker's equipment. But attention is now concentrated on sensitivity, his awareness of the changing needs of the young people with whom he works.

c A related aspect of the last point is 'objectivity and self-awareness'. Like many other folk, youth workers are often the last to be aware of their own faults. Favouritism or paternalism or impatience—may be obvious to all except the worker who displays these unhelpful traits. Social workers of all kinds need to be able continually to assess themselves without destroying their self-confidence. Ways and means have been encouraged—supervision is one (see *e*)—of helping youth workers 'to see ourselves as others see us'.

d The 'new' approach to leadership has had its effect on the shape and content of training courses. They have become more 'non-directed' in the negative sense that it is no longer assumed that a tutor knows all the answers which he passes on and positively, in the sense that the student is encouraged to describe his own training needs and how they can be met: the student has been enabled to take a more active part in his own training. It has been said that 'all training is self-training'. Consistent with this is the aim of the course to provide experiences for the student that will be the basis of his own further reflection and in some cases, to expose him to a discovery of his own need for further skill. Practical work with a youth group is an essential part of this process and leads to the seminar on general theories. Moreover, this takes place in a small group with a tutor, not in a large classroom with a lecturer. And there is time for personal tutorials.

e Lastly, stress has been laid on the need to see training as a continual process, for professionals and part-timers alike. Nobody ought ever to say that he has 'done youth leadership' just as a man with a degree in psychology ought not to say he has 'done psychology'. And though this relates to gathering more information and keeping up with developments in the field, yet the ongoing process of training has been most closely linked with 'supervision'. (The word represents an unfortunate choice—Youth Service labours to find the right vocabulary—suggesting an 'overseer' which is not at all the idea.) The process presupposes that the worker keeps a record of what happens in the youth group session, writing down, as soon after the session as possible, his observations of the most important events in relation to the group as a whole, sub-groups, individuals and himself as the leader. The recording is a tool for the job—it is an *aide mémoire*—and also a tool for further training. He can reflect upon it afterwards. If he is fortunate, he will have a 'supervisor' who will act as a sounding board when he reflects aloud upon the items on the recording; a 'supervisor' who may say 'And what happened next?' and 'What did you make of that?' or even 'Are you sure you were right when you. . . ?', but never 'What I say about situations like that is. . . .' In fact, it is the first process, of vigorous self-examination, which can be hopefully encouraged.

'Supervision' is only one, though the most discussed, of the aspects of the continued process of training. Youth work contains within itself, like many other human activities, the challenge of an inherent excellence and people usually either become more skilful or more slipshod.

No doubt the list sounds idealistic, especially to hard-pressed practitioners and it is a statement which attempts to summarize the best intentions. But there can be little doubt that on the whole these developments helped to raise the standards of youth work during this period. They disturbed the complacency, challenged the paternalism (which is only authoritarianism with a conscience) and upset the 'personality-cult' of many who needed these abrasive services. It was wholly good in its stress on sensitivity, on the leader's need for self-examination and for training courses which could be tested by their production of efficiency in the task of the social education of young people. If anybody doubts this, he should read some of the books that were being written on the subject twenty-five years ago. They make youth work have an undue reliance upon the personal qualities of the leader, not realizing that leadership is at least as much a product of the situation as it is of personality. Most of them contained a discouraging list of 'qualities needed by the leader'. As late as 1948 we find one writer urging, 'Youth leaders need to be shop-windows through which young people can see and admire all that is good and worthwhile.' In commenting on this statement, Davies and Gibson write, 'The assumption that youth workers themselves offer perfect models of good social development has remained undisturbed in much modern youth work.'[26]

But though the general effect of the 'new approaches' has been good, yet one has several misgivings about them: mostly about the way in which they have been presented. Technical terms have given some voluntary workers an intellectual inferiority complex. 'Acceptance' has taken the place of 'caring' and 'conversation' has been replaced by 'dialogue'. Sometimes the whole operation has been made to appear too difficult for ordinary folk who after all provide the bulk of the support. Questionings of motives have disturbed the introspective and given rise to guilt feelings. Nobody has bothered to say that within wide limits it does not matter what motives you start with so long as you will allow them to be modified with experience of the work. (There is a true, cautionary tale of a girl, happily working with a youth group, who joined a training course to improve her skill. She found herself surprisingly in a situation where her motives were attacked in the presence of others, and she was challenged to 'self-awareness'. This was supposed to be 'abrasive therapy'. She gave up the course in alarm.) The advocates of new approaches have not always proved to be good communicators or even good educators, finding out where people are and meeting them there and building further knowledge and insight on what they have already.

Moreover, the new approaches are not without their dangers and possible deficiencies, which is to say no more than that they share the common lot of all approaches. In teaching new techniques, they run the risk of increasing the self-consciousness of the worker and decreasing his spontaniety. 'Social group method' may lead to verbalization, the use of new words rather than the use of a new and exact technique.

In the matter of personal qualities, one wonders if the pendulum has not swung too far in the direction of a detached and 'professional' attitude. Of course everybody would agree that ideally one should have the right mixture of both; presumably the perfect youth leader would include among his virtues something of the warmth of a friend, and something of the precision of a scientist. But emphasis swings from one to the other and perhaps the time has come to redress the balance in favour of character traits: compassion does not have to be patronizing. Paul Halmos has shown that, however detached the social worker thinks himself to be, he is usually supported by a philosophy and often uses the disguised language of love.[27] Robin Guthrie once conducted a survey in Liverpool in public houses among former members of boys' clubs: he found that what they remembered most was the personality of the leader, and in particular, his friendship and affection.[28]

Experience in training encourages one to look again at the dangerous half-truth 'leaders are born not made'. At least when candidates present themselves for training, their characters are set in a way that will seriously affect the work they do with young people. Most importantly, they are by this time either caring people who feel what is happening to others and have a desire to help—or they are not: and in the latter case, training is unlikely to change them.

'Personality of workers' probably counts for more in youth work than in other branches of educational and social work for a variety of reasons. (Years ago, Macalister Brew gave 'Don't be afraid to use your personality' as one of the commandments for leaders.) The first is that he works with no captive audience and one of the factors which decides whether the youngster stays with him or not is his own personality: a warm, interesting and lively person will tend to hold their interest longer than a cold, dull and lifeless alternative. (Anybody who has worked with a youth group for a few months knows this to be true. Every employing body knows it, and will properly ask questions about the personality of candidates for an appointment. It is only worth mentioning here because some writers on the subject seem to deny it by inference or at least to minimize it.) The second reason is that more than others the youth worker often has room 'to do his job in his own way': he has, relatively, freedom for self-interpretation of his role: he can often be an innovator, not simply a routinee. This is partly because other people involved in the work may not be clear what are its objectives: there are not clear expectations of youth work and youth workers. This may be a source of weakness since it reduces support but it does mean that he has more hand in interpretation of his efforts; he is an artist, not a copy typist. If this is the situation, personal qualities are important.

What has been said applies both to voluntary and professional workers for their goal and methods should not differ in essentials. But of course their own situation differs. The professional has spent a longer time in training and should have more expertise, do more work and carry more responsibility. Moreover if there is a clash with the authorities who are the controlling body, and if they have expectations which conflict with his values and intentions, then he has more to lose by having the courage of his own convictions. It is not suggested that this is the usual situation, but it has been known to occur and the full-time youth worker discovers that it is true for him as for others, that nobody gives him freedom: he either acts as a free man, or in allowing social pressures to override his integrity, he is guilty of what Sartre calls 'bad faith'. To suggest that Youth Service is a profession only for heroes and saints is unrealistic: but one example has been given of the need for strength of purpose and self-confidence: and in the light of this, and similar situations, to suggest that personal qualities are unimportant is ludicrous. The successful operator uses rather than suppresses his personality whilst checking any tendency to be subjective in his judgements or to be unconsciously satisfying his own needs rather than the needs of young people in his efforts.

What follows claims to have a present reference. It is certainly not an attempt to produce a new list of 'qualities needed by the leader'. Rather, on the basis of one man's observations reinforced and constantly modified by many discussions, it is a short account of those qualities which at present are conspicuously lacking, yet which would, if they were present, be most rewarding for the social education of many youngsters in our country.

1 First, there is 'imagination'. This is simply an ability to see what might be for the organization and the members. It is linked with that undiscouragable faith in people's possibilities which is the mark of the true educator; about the good youth leader as he looks at the young people there is something reminiscent of the prospector's remark, 'There's gold in them thar hills'. Many of the conspicuous examples of success in youth work go back to an original piece of imaginative insight of a worker. The most commonly quoted examples are where a club member has been encouraged to discover his educational possibilities and climb the social ladder. Appreciation, friendship and imagination of youth workers helped an errand boy to become the principal of a college of education, a junior clerk to become a parson, and a boy working on a bread delivery van to aspire to be a commercial artist. But those are not the commonest, nor the most impressive examples. Many more youngsters have been helped by the same original act of faith to be mature adults with a co-operative independence, able to develop enduring and affectionate personal relationships, with wider interests and a new self-confidence.

A generation ago, L. J. Barnes criticized the 'indoctrinators' in youth work and compared them unfavourably with 'the facilitators'.[29] His strictures were justified since, as we have seen, adult people are prone to think that they know what is good for the young. 'Do not rescue me prematurely,' said an Arctic explorer as he disappeared into the icy wastes and perhaps, to adults, many young people would use the same phrase if they knew it. Yet the 'indoctrinator' is not as common as the worker, who, through lack of imagination, simply does not have enough ideas.

Youth workers have to create and maintain interest, but they are not likely to do this if they are not interested or interesting. Imagination links with the specific skill of informal education, of being able to tempt youngsters to become involved in an area of knowledge or skill, that left alone, they would not choose for themselves.

> Men must be taught
> As if you taught them not.
> And things unknown proposed
> As things forgot.

2   The second necessary quality is the ability to work as a member of a team. There are still too many 'lone wolves'; too many leaders who cannot delegate real responsibility, who have apparently not heard that 'a leader is not a man who does ten men's work but who persuades ten men to work'. There are still many youth enterprises where there is no attempt to have a regular staff meeting (or if there is, it is not an example of genuine co-operative thinking and planning): and apparently the only time the helpers meet is when they are on the job.

Important for all, this again is crucial for the professionals. Their role is diverse and can include administration, case work, group work, public relations and education: only a rare versatility can do well in all of those. At least one may persuade others to do what one is not able to do oneself.

Individualists who cannot work happily as members of a team are denying possibilities to the young people with whom they work.

3   Lastly, there is the ability to grow as people with the work we are doing. Personal involvement with a youth group challenges our immaturity, self-centredness, insularity, prejudices, temerity and sloth. (Years ago, a girl of narrow evangelical views began to work in a club because, as she said, 'It will bring me in touch with young people who can be converted.' Months later a friend asked how she was faring. 'It's a funny thing,' she replied, 'but I have come to like these young people so much as they are now that I am not sure I want to see them converted.') Youth work can be a liberal and personal education. No man is left unaffected by it. But if we do not grow into bigger people, we may diminish: certainly our usefulness is related to our own personal development.

The best hope of improvement is in the increase of the skill of the shop floor workers: and the relevant features of an increase of skill would be imagination, team work and personal development.

THE NEEDIEST NOT SERVED

John Wesley, the founder of the Methodist movement, sternly admonished his early preachers, 'Go not to those who need you, but to those who need you most.' It is necessary counsel for all who organize voluntary movements which rely upon constant renewal and recruitment from outside themselves: for the missionary impulse weakens. When the days of the first fine careless rapture are over, the movement becomes an organization and passes into a more defensive phase. Organizations tend to become more interested in themselves as time passes; hence they begin to make rules for consolidation and stability rather than recruitment; and so they develop out-group attitudes and value loyalty and conformity among their members.

To this general rule, British Youth Service—which is made up of a number of organizations, statutory and voluntary—is no exception. It is natural and expected that 'a good club member' or a boy who is 'keen on the Brigade' will be valued above the apathetic youngster. The adults who work in these organizations need to win the approval of others—senior officers and to some extent, the general public—to sustain the work and their own position. A contemporary example of the point can be found in the Youth Service of Jamaica.[30] A feature of the work in that island is the establishment of residential camps providing for hundreds of youths who are illiterate, unskilled and unemployed. For years now the basis of entry to the camp has been need alone and the enterprise has catered for the most seriously under-privileged youth of Jamaica. But at the present time, the organizers of the camp are under pressure to apply literacy tests for candidates and thus to replace the criterion of need by one of merit: the results would be so much more impressive, it is felt, if this step were taken.

All youth movements become more respectable as time goes on. This process can even be observed within the short history of one unit. A club which recruits rough, undisciplined boys may find in a few years' time that those same boys are the chief obstacle to recruiting another generation of rough boys: the first set have now become the Establishment: there is nobody quite so Pharisaical as the reformed Publican.

Nationally, the effects of this development are seen in a service about which it has sometimes been said that it has little appeal for those who most need it. The phrase refers to those who have come to be called 'the unattached' which is intended to describe, not merely those who do not join existing youth organizations, but youngsters who seem to be experiencing above-average difficulty in growing into mature adults and adjusting to society: they are often bored, frequently lack social confidence, experience difficulty in establishing stable relationships, do not settle down to a steady job, and are sometimes near-delinquent: the usual sources of socialization have proved inadequate in their case. Mary Morse wrote, '. . . the vast majority of the unattached youth contacted would scorn membership of any kind of youth organization. But far from spending their time in any demonstrably constructive fashion, they were manifestly unhappy and frequently delinquent.'

Not everybody would agree that the 'unattached' (in the sense in which the term has been defined above) are the proper concern of Youth Service. There are those who think that the disturbed or mal-adjusted youngsters in our society are the responsibility of one of the specialist social work agencies. For themselves they see Youth Service as an aspect of educational service and taking place in an educational establishment. Others press the point further. They believe that in recent years, we have been so fascinated by the glamour of work among the 'unattached', that we have neglected to learn how to 'liberate' those who are 'attached'. The sheep in the fold are untended whilst we go off on the exciting search for the sheep lost on the hills.

We touch here on one of the deep divisions of opinion among those who work with young people in their leisure-time. Sufficient, at the moment, to say that most of these points seem to be covered if it is recognized that we are pleading for a Youth Service with a variety of provisions designed to meet the needs of different types of youngsters —the grammar school youngster no less than the frustrated youngster who may soon be tempted to express his frustration in acts of vandalism.

Among those youngsters who seem to be at odds with their society, there are two broad types. The first, in a sense, are 'too good for society' as it is now. They are criticizing some feature of their society —its violence or artificiality or insincerity. They are the 'socially-rejecting'. After all, Socrates was alienated from society, but for good reasons. The second are 'not good enough for society' in the sense that they cannot receive the 'good things' their society is offering to them, though admittedly in other ways, it may be denying them 'good things' and in this sense they are the 'socially-rejected'. As we have seen, they have been called the 'unattached'; for Goetschius and Tash they are the 'can't copes': James Hemming once referred to them as 'the desocialized'.

To write in this way about any group of human beings too easily gives the impression of being clinical, impersonal and patronizing. It is justified only by the conviction that a contribution can thereby be made to the understanding of young people who could be enriched

G

by Youth Service but are not at the moment attracted by its provisions.

What can we say about the 'unattached'?

First, that they are frequently educational 'drop-outs'. They have usually been bored in their last months at school; they do not usually continue their education after 15; they make a limited response to life's interests: they are emotionally immature; often in an inarticulate way, they realize they are not very clever in a world where the individual's social importance is measured by his cleverness.

But though this is a common feature widely distributed among the 'unattached', they are not all the same in every respect: at least three distinct groups can be discerned.

1　There are those who respond to their frustration with apathy and listlessness. In a world of wonders, they are bored. An expensive educational system has not given them the self-confidence to make the most of themselves. The sad truth is that they are passing through one of the formative periods of human development, without the personal growth which can enrich the rest of their lives. Stanley Hall wrote that the purpose of adolescence is to irrigate old age. Conversely, a 'bad' adolescence is one which fails to lay the foundations for a more enjoyable adult life.

2　Then there are those 'unattached' youngsters who react in more aggressive and often delinquent ways. The case-histories from the various experimental projects among the 'unattached' frequently reveal the resentment and a bitterness of those who feel they have been let down and are determined to get their own back. This may go back to their early experiences in the family—they found indifference and neglect where they confidently looked for love. Or it may be that in their present struggles for identity and significance, they feel that everyman's hand is against them. There are many reasons for the increase of juvenile delinquency in modern industrial communities. We do not find one single psychological or sociological explanation. But Cohen's views have received strong support.[31] He believes that the delinquency of lower class boys is primarily a way of achieving status by illegal means because it is denied to them by a society dominated by middle class standards.

3　Finally, there are the more seriously disturbed youngsters—addicted to hard drugs, or incorrigibly criminal or anarchistic. Some of them are retreatists who have withdrawn from society: others have declared a personal war on society, whilst receiving its benefits when they themselves are distressed. They are of course, as are the other groups described in this section, a minority. But there is plenty of evidence that there are a significant number of youngsters at risk in a society like ours. 'Rootless in cities' showed that every conurbation is likely to include a number of these 'lost adolescents'. Goetschius and Tash found them in Paddington. The Seebohm Committee reported the need for more provision in psychiatric hospitals for severely disturbed adolescents.

For this last group, Youth Service has a limited relevance, certainly as Youth Service is organized today in its conventional forms. An adequate provision might have 'kept those youngsters from falling' but as they are now, they need specialist help.

To the first two groups, Youth Service has much to offer, in prevention, care and inspiration, through its educational and pastoral approaches. A 'good' youth group has been described as a place where an adolescent boy (or girl) can find four things.

1   He is valued as a human being, for what he is now, not only for what he may become.
2   He is tempted, though not coerced, to take up new interests.
3   He has a hand in the running of the show and can influence policy if he wants to.
4   There is an attentive adult ear if he wants to talk over a personal problem.

Though this is admittedly to describe the youth group in ideal terms, yet even an approximation to these standards would have meaning for the 'unattached' particularly those in the first two groups: if the educational and pastoral intentions of Youth Service are carried out, it has much to offer the alienated. Informal methods of education, for example, can be for many youngsters the most effective methods of further education, persuading them that the worlds of knowledge and art and activity are not closed to them and only open to the 'clever and sophisticated'. An effective provision could also convince many of them that it is not necessary to accept everything uncritically in one's society to be a citizen; that one can be a radical and a revolutionary without being an anarchist or a nihilist; that personal frustrations and deprivations can be worked out in more constructive ways than bitterness and resentment. For them, as for many others, one of the main purposes of Youth Service is to demonstrate that you can have a lot more fun in a lot more places, without spoiling anybody else's fun.

But for the most part the 'unattached' remain obstinately unattached. The commonest customer is the secondary modern youngster in the upper streams of the school; the appeal to the conformist and immature is strong, to the rebellious and anti-social it is minimal.

We have already suggested some of the reasons why this is so from the point of view of the workers and organizers. Conformists give better support and are associated with measurable signs of success—classes attended, trophies won, discipline and responsibility. A response from the 'unattached' is harder to win. Nobody who wants a quiet life and a successful career will work with them. It is tempting to take the line of least resistance.

To this must be added, resistance which arises from the way in which the young 'unattached' is likely to see the Service. It will almost certainly have a juvenile image for him. There is plenty of evidence that he rejects it as 'kid's stuff', not very different from school which he has thankfully escaped. Consistently, he will see it as representing the values of a society which he rejects, at least partly, representing 'They' rather than 'Us'; on the side of adults and the middle-classes. Detached workers among the 'unattached' have faced an acute dilemma. How far could they be 'non-judgmental' in their dealings with the young people they contacted? If they simply represented the middle-class values with which most of them grew up, they were in danger of losing touch with the clients; if they went too far in accepting the standards of the clients, they were in danger of forfeiting their own integrity and even of themselves being in trouble with the police. For Goetschius and Tash this is 'the problem of identity' for the detached youth worker.

This is a disabling difficulty and may further confirm some in the conviction that Youth Service has nothing to offer to the severely alienated youngster in our society. We must work with the sanctions of law and order and be seen to be agents of socialization. The issue is not settled so simply or so hopelessly. The dilemma in fact represents one of the possible growing points for Youth Service, though not without pain.

Elsewhere in this work we have argued the need for a broad philosophy for Youth Service. The suggestion was made that the primary purpose is the critical involvement of young people in their society. Some such definition needs to be discussed regularly in the local youth group—at the meetings of the management committee, at the members' committee, between the leader and his adult workers and informally among the members. 'What are we trying to do?' will usually introduce new ideas to some. They may come to see that simply providing well-drilled youngsters or a strong organization is not enough: that there are sanctions for the work other than those given by the Law and public opinion. Fortunately we are not confronted with a straight choice between being 'non-judgmental' and being 'judgment-loaded': there are middle positions to be usefully occupied which still allow young people large areas of self-determination without cutting themselves off from adult counsel.

There are certainly one or two refreshing instances in the country where the consultation and teamwork we have been describing has led to a change in the image of a particular youth organization. The reflection upon the purpose of the enterprise has led to an acceptance of responsibility for the social education of youngsters in a neighbourhood rather than for a successful organization in a building. Though the two aims are often complementary, there are incidents when they are in conflict with each other and a choice has to be made. It would not be fair to suggest that the image can always be changed without opposition, particularly from those who, perhaps unconsciously, are hoping to recruit the worthiest rather than the neediest.

The outreach of the youth organization could be increased by two further improvements. The first is by an enhancement of the counselling skills of those who work there. What is wanted is not the professional caseworker in the youth group, but more adult workers who are capable of listening, giving objective advice and being resource people when the youngster needs the help of a specialist agency. The second is by having greater variety in the programme of activities, hence providing a wider appeal. Existing youth organizations could serve the 'unattached' far more efficiently than at present. But in addition we need more detached workers who will make contact with youngsters outside youth organizations with no strings of membership or commitment attaching to the work. The few experiments so far in this field have uncovered the need rather than met it. Money is short today for all kinds of educational and social work but though it is hard to measure the success of the detached worker, yet the fact is that if he kept two boys per year out of Borstal by his efforts, he would be making a profit for public funds.

NEW AND BETTER FORMS OF PARTNERSHIP

Like many other institutions, Youth Service shows a fondness for words which evoke reverence beyond their deserts—if measured by achievement: one such word in this case is 'partnership'. In practice, the thought is usually of co-operation between government (local and national) and voluntary agencies: it is mostly confined to the ideal of common effort among those engaged in 'Official Youth Service'. Our present consideration will be largely confined to this area though we have shown that our own hope is for a 'Youth Service' which becomes 'youth work' and is seen to occur in many places and takes many forms and therefore involves partnership with people who are not directly concerned with youth movements. If this hope is fulfilled, the old boundaries of 'Youth Service' will disappear. But at best, this process will take some time. Meanwhile, young people might be better served if there was a more effective partnership among those who work in youth organizations.

One does not wish to minimize the achievements of that partnership which began with the issue of circular 1486 in November 1939 by (the then) Board of Education. Prompted by the knowledge that the war would involve the total population and family life would be disrupted, the authorities encouraged a partnership in the service of youth between statutory bodies and voluntary organizations. '. . . The Board of Education shall undertake a direct responsibility for youth welfare. . . . The Board, therefore, urge that all local education authorities for higher education should now take steps to see that properly constituted Youth Committees shall exist in their areas.'[32] This step has not lacked high praise: it has been described as heralding a new chapter in British social history and as the most decisive step in modern British Youth Service: circular 1486 and circular 1516 (which followed soon afterwards) have been called 'the Bible of British Youth Service'.

There can be no doubt that much of value has followed for the youth of the nation. Douglas Hubery[33] has outlined the four main areas in which the partnership has worked:

1 In the organization of Youth Service itself. Cities like Birmingham and Liverpool have seen the strengthening of the voluntary organizations by statutory help; areas where voluntary organizations were weak have seen the opening of civic youth centres.

2   In the sharing of leaders: voluntary workers have been enlisted for civic centres: where necessary public funds have supported part-time paid or full-time leaders in voluntary centres.
3   There has been partnership in training of part-time workers.
4   There has been financial support from public funds for equipment and running expenses as well as for leaders.

Nevertheless, the partnership has not been without its tensions: they were present in the earliest days and some of them continue to the present time. To begin with, there was an early unjustified fear that it was the intention of the authorities to set up a National Youth Service. There is every indication that the originators would have abhorred any such development. A National Youth Committee was at first proposed but this was thought to be reminiscent of a State-directed movement, though both interests were to be represented: by 1942 this had been replaced by the Youth Advisory Council. A more conspicuous example of the government's rejection of a totalitarian movement was the matter of the registration of young people. The plans were announced in 1941 and the registration took place in 1942 and 1943. All boys between 16 and 17 were required to register, but the subsequent interview was voluntary and as news of this spread, less and less boys presented themselves for the interview. 'Compulsory interviewing was never adopted because it would have destroyed the essential freedom of the Youth Service.'[34] Fears of a national and nationalistic youth movement sponsored by the authorities have long been allayed: but other early fears are with us in new forms.

Thus, despite many areas of co-operation, both between organizations and individuals, and indeed an expansion of the work of voluntary organizations, there has always been a lingering fear that the statutory body, in some areas at least, might be making a 'take-over bid' for Youth Service: there have always been those who saw the partnership as containing elements of threat. This misgiving has been fed by certain realities. After circular 1486, many full-time workers in voluntary organizations transferred to statutory service and this at a time when manpower was short in war-time conditions. Statutory authorities control the purse-strings and though their support has been appreciated, it puts the voluntary organizations in the position of going 'cap in hand'; in some areas it has been felt that authorities are far more concerned to foster their own schemes than help those of others.

On the local authority side there has been a feeling not without substance, that some voluntary organizations are inefficient, centres of entrenched traditionalism and emotional vested interests. (Compare the true story of the secretary of the church youth organization who was in a muddle through not answering letters or keeping copies. Asked to do better she replied, 'But that would be efficiency and we don't want that spirit, do we?') They suspect them of overlapping of staff, old-fashioned methods and outlook and tribal loyalty to the movement in which they have spent their lives. One or two wild statements made in the early days by local government officials (such as the declared aim 'to wipe the inefficient voluntary organizations off the map') have rankled.

To some this will seem like ancient history but there are too many places where the partnership between voluntary and statutory agencies contains elements of an uneasy alliance. In recent years, the joint training of part-time workers has been undertaken but nobody could say that it worked everywhere as well as it might have done, and there can be no doubt that the main reason was that the two partners did not trust each other fully.

In saying that people from different backgrounds and varying positions do not always work in the closest harmony—though they both serve the same section of the population—one is only describing a common human situation. People *are* liable to feel under threat: their own success, status and self-esteem *is* bound up with the success of the work they do for others: they *do* manifest a tendency to believe that this way is the only way. Yet the consequences of defective partnership are serious. At its worst, the situation is one more illustration of the way in which young people may suffer loss because older people fail to understand each other. We cannot rise to the task and the opportunities unless in British Youth Service, we have joint use of resources both physical and human, and joint planning for the social education of the young. We can afford and must have variety in Youth Service: we cannot afford fragmentation of effort.

Some of the issues of partnership depend on what is done about various recent reports on the structure of local government (Maud) social services (Seebohm) and community work (Gulbenkian). Whatever happens, however, much of the issue will be decided by those who work at whatever level in 'Youth Service'. It is easy to point to a theoretical statement of the condition of an even more fruitful partnership. Each side must simply see what the other has to give. In summary, this means statutory authorities appreciating that voluntary organizations are an aspect of community involvement, that they often are more flexible and because they are not directly spending public money can afford to experiment, as they have done notably in the last ten years. (One wishes that there were more educational officials like the one quoted by Macalister Brew who said that if he were to undertake club work he could not hope to provide anything as good as the best voluntary club, but he could not tolerate anything as bad as the worst.)[35] Workers in voluntary organizations *can* be insular and anxious: they need to recognize that a local authority has a responsibility for all the youngsters, many of whom will not be attracted to a favourite movement, however worthy and time-honoured. But one realizes that in asking flesh and blood to put the needs of young people always first, one is asking a lot: it calls for a measure of generosity, tolerance and confidence at every level, from the youth officer of a large authority to a man running a one-night-a-week-club: it is in fact one more illustration of the fact that moral and spiritual appeals are inseparable from an improved youth work in Britain.

There are other partners than Youth Service officials and youth workers. One thinks of teachers, for example. There is a welcome change, due no doubt partly to the many youth work courses at colleges of education, but there are still some teachers who think of youth work as necessarily an inferior form of education, since it often lacks an obvious and measurable purpose. One thinks too of councillors who may be members of education committees and work to a philosophy of 'no money for fun', for whom Youth Service is an immediate and obvious target for cuts in days of economy, since in their eyes it represents the 'frills'. And, of course, one looks beyond educational service. A few years ago, conducting a joint seminar for Youth Employment Officers and full-time youth leaders and officers, the writer was horrified to discover how little real knowledge each had of the other's intentions and duties.

'Partnership' then has received much lip-service: and it has impressive achievements to its credit; but we are only at the beginning of the discovery of what effective partnership could accomplish for the social education of many adolescents in Britain.

INFORMED PUBLIC SUPPORT

One frequently hears the complaint that there is little interest in, information about, and support for youth movements among the general public. It is the second of those which is basic. There is certainly much interest in young people in our society but it is most quickly evoked when they are reported as having done something spectacularly bad or spectacularly good—a fact which is well appre-cited by those responsible for the mass media of communication. There are, it is true, a minority of adults who take a jaundiced view of Youth Service because they have a jaundiced view of young people. But on the whole any charge that our society is not interested in the young and what they do is hard to support. On the whole, too, there is general support for youth movements. Parents, for example, are likely to consider them a good thing.

But the reasons for this general and, it must be admitted, often tepid and passive support are usually not very satisfactory. To begin with it is strongly based on the belief that youth movements have mainly a custodial function. 'Well, I suppose it keeps them off the streets' can still be heard from well-meaning people who support the work, verbally and from outside. The commonest expectation is that the building of a new centre will be followed by a decrease of delin-quency and vandalism in the neighbourhood—an expectation, by the way, which is sometime fulfilled. For many people the pictures which the words 'Youth Service' brings on are 'Boy Scouts', 'dancing and table tennis' or 'clubs'. Recently, a new image has been contributed by some (not all) television programmes in which youth workers appear. Here they are depicted as sentimental, soft-headed people who believe that the most incorrigible young thug can be changed by kindness and understanding. In the story, they are shown to be wrong by the tough treatment of a police-sergeant, or strangely enough, a realistic curate from a working-class background.

What is not widely appreciated are the more sophisticated aims which have been hammered out through persistent failures. 'The Youth Service . . . provides for the continued social and informal education of young people in terms most likely to bring them to maturity, those of responsible personal choice,' says the Albemarle Report. Everybody who knows the inside story would agree that in many places the words are a hopeful prophecy about the future, rather than an accurate des-cription of the present. But those words briefly summarize the best intentions. That Youth Service strives to help young people to stand on their own feet in an increasingly complex human situation; that it seeks to supply the materials and experience from which they can make a married relationship which will provide not only stability, but enduring fun; that it wants to open their eyes to those wonders of life and the earth which they are capable of appreciating but which they could pass through their lives unheeding—these are a few of the aims which are not widely appreciated.

The groaners are right if they complain that benign salutations based on imperfect knowledge and understanding are not enough.[36] One reason is that this attitude will not command the financial resources that are required, neither from voluntary subscriptions nor from public funds. It is noticeable that when a local authority cuts expenditure on Youth Service, there is little public outcry: protests come only from those within the service. Few candidates at local or parliamentary elections bother to mention youth work in their manifestoes. These things can only be because there is a widespread failure to appreciate the urgency and the promise of the social education of the young.

Moreover, benign salutations will not gather sufficient, nor always the right kind of workers to staff the work. Busy men and women may hesitate to volunteer to spend hours every week 'keeping them off the streets' when their companions tell them that a commercial dance hall could achieve this goal more effectively and with less cost in blood, sweat and tears. And youth work in this country needs more volunteers from the ranks of professional and business men. This is not to denigrate the many hundreds of non-professional and non-business men—'the not many mighty, not many noble'—who have been included among those who volunteered for training and service in the last ten years. Many of them would be the first to admit that the training has been an important aspect of their own further education. It is simply that the work demands the help of all types to be effective. Even in those cases where people have volunteered because they feel their own lives were empty, this is not, of course, a motive to be rejected: it can, as has been demonstrated over and over again, lead to good workers. But we also need busy people, whose lives are full, but who find room for *this* because its urgency and promise are seen. The implications of this view are discussed in later chapters.

No less important is a third reason why benign, ill-informed support is inadequate. This is summarized in a U.N.E.S.C.O. report,[37] '. . . the essential point is that the whole of society, through its various structures—political and social, governmental and non-governmental, educational and spiritual—should become aware of the problems of youth.' For us, this should mean that Youth Service shares with other agencies the responsibility to change and improve the attitudes of the whole society to the young. Perhaps it has a reforming function that does not always belong to related social work agencies, for some of which it makes sense to say that its officers are 'social workers, not social reformers' (though outside their office, they may of course be involved in revolutionary movements). But Youth Service cannot be said to have done its work when it has established a plethora of well-run, well-attended organizations; nor even when it has enthused an army of workers in those organizations; it has a function outside itself. It contributes to a society where it is commoner for adults to take an unfussy, non-interfering interest in what happens to young people: caring, but rigorously refusing to trespass on the integrity, independence and individuality of each adolescent; wanting them to be enriched by the ages but insisting that they find the treasure for themselves.

Forty years ago, apprentices in the steel mills at Sheffield could face unpleasantness in their first days at work. But there were at least some older men who saw themselves with a responsibility for the youngsters, not only to pass on their skills but also to protect them against any corrupting influences: over-protection was ruled out by the nature of the case. No apology is made for the view that the widespread adoption of the modern counterpart of this attitude is one of the ultimate aims of Youth Service. But it can scarcely be said to be meeting with success, if these wider aims are not understood or appreciated.

Why is this so? Those involved in youth work may be tempted, in a self-pitying mood, to blame circumstances, society and the 'original sin' of the people. Popular newspapers are indicted because of their fondness for reporting youthful crimes on the basis that 'man-bites-dog' is news. But aside from the fact that this is not always fair, youth workers need to remind themselves that like everybody else, they have to work with the world as it is and not 'to fancy what were fair provided it could be'. Nobody owes Youth Service a living. Much of the bad publicity we have received and the inadequate public image we conjure up, is our own fault.

So we return to a repeated theme. This again is a plea against insularity. Youth work must never be seen in isolation from the community. Every youth group should be so to speak on the highway. And this means that attention must be given to public relationships. Local education committees and officials have an educational task about Youth Service with all the people in their area: local leaders and workers have a task to communicate to the world outside the unit what they intend and what they do, and this not only to the parents of their members.

Whilst it would be unfair to deny that many do attend to the public relationships aspect, yet the long list of missed opportunities and faulty communications are depressing. There are unattractive brochures and posters; failure to use the local newspaper, often enough eager to be used; failure to involve a wide cross-section of the public in the work. It is not without significance that, as we have seen, the Albemarle suggestion of Supporters' clubs for youth ventures fell dead from the printer's hand. Youth workers must be prepared to talk about what they are doing and they should learn to do this unselfishly, non-glamorously and hopefully; they can learn also to be 'wise as serpents, harmless as doves' by beginning with the notions people have about Youth Service—as for example, that it is an anti-delinquency enterprise—and then move quickly on to show that it has other, wider and even more important objectives.

A CADRE OF PROFESSIONAL WORKERS

Contrary to popular belief, the professional youth worker is not always a club leader; he may be a group worker in a coffee bar or a street worker; the term can be stretched to include Area Youth Organizer or even Youth Officer. But the commonest type at present is the club or centre warden.

The Albemarle Report found it necessary to justify the existence of the full-time worker.

It is not enough to prove that the full-time leader can justify his day. We must be satisfied too that a corps of such people is for the good of the Service. We are convinced that it is. A youth leader of the kind we are thinking of can bring a trained mind to bear on needs and problems of the young worker: he can experiment with new techniques and new modes of youth work: and he can give the time to planning and preparation that will enable him to make plain the standards of achievement that can be reached in informal group work. In all three capacities, as a student of adolescence at first hand, as an innovator, and as a demonstrator of the possibilities of

the medium, he can have an influence far beyond his own
club; and a strong body of such skilled workers is indispensable
if the standards of the Service are to be raised.[38]

Not every professional youth worker has since justified his own
existence in these terms; nor has every one been allowed to do so;
but there would be general agreement that there is a place for the
full-time operator for the reasons Albemarle Report gives. A Service
which will continue to lean heavily on 'spare-time' help will need a
cadre of professionals.

Yet perhaps there is no subject in Youth Service which has led
to such prolonged and often heated discussion in the last ten years.
Part of the trouble is that there is not in our society a clear consensus
of role expectations for the professional youth worker. In most of
the jobs that people do, they are guided in their performance by what
is expected of them. The vast majority of the population have a clear
idea how doctors, teachers, parsons, nurses, dustmen and bus con-
ductors ought to do their work; and generally these expectations are
fulfilled. These jobs and many like them are defined for a number
of reasons. One is that the people who do these jobs are widely spread
throughout the community and most of us come into contact with
them at some time or other and receive their services; another is that
most of them are long-established jobs; a third is that there are not
wide regional variations in the way these workers are expected to
perform—a nurse in Devon and a nurse on Tyneside, for example, are
subject to much the same expectations; finally, most of us either know
that we need the services of these workers—as in the case of a doctor
—or we are compelled to use them—as in the case of a teacher.

If the list is examined in relation to the professional youth worker,
it will be found that none of the four conditions apply for him. There
are comparatively few of them, less than 1% say of the number of
teachers there are in the country; in a sense it is a comparatively new
profession; there are big variations between their jobs in different parts
of the country; young people use their services voluntarily and they
are not driven to them by urgent and claimant needs. Hence the
question is still asked, 'What does the full-time club leader do in the
daytime?' Within the Service itself there has been a continuing discussion on the theme, 'Is the professional youth worker an educator
or a social worker?' He tends to be a marginal man among community workers. One of the difficulties in the training is that one

can never be quite sure of the situation to which the student will go on the completion of his course, depending on the expectations in his first appointment and new emphases in the Service as a whole. (One comment from a former student in her first job was that she wished the course had included shorthand and typing; another observer remarked that no such course was complete unless it included a large section on Chinese civilization.) Today, there are properly new demands in the stress on seeing young people as part of, and not isolated from, the community; the 'youth worker' has now become a 'youth and community worker'.

This uncertainty of role has had important results. Whilst it may be true that those whose role is not defined have more freedom for self-interpretation, this has proved to be a doctrine better suited to the outstanding leaders; those with less gifts and self-confidence have sometimes found the lack of support, knowledge and expectations a source of anxiety and isolation. In a few cases they have demonstrated the maxim that those whose jobs gain little prestige, go looking for prestige.

There is a need for rethinking the role of the full-time youth worker, both at national and many local levels. The Albemarle paragraph has to be spelt out in greater detail. And with this, of course, is related the rethinking and restructuring of the whole Service such as we have been suggesting. The various points at this level are as follows and it is only fair to say that they receive careful consideration in the new policy statement from the Youth Service Development Council.[39]

1 *Adequate salary and career structure* Unless this comes to pass we shall simply not attract the calibre of person required.
2 *More assistants' posts* It is unrealistic to expect most youngsters to come out of college and take charge of an organization which may have 300 members, and where he or she will be the only professional worker regularly on the premises.
3 *Larger training courses* For nine years Westhill College of Education has held the only two-year course. During that period the National College at Leicester has been the biggest provider and the course there has been one year. Their success is a tribute to the devotion and skill of the staff, but now as the new report says, 'The one year courses impose strain on both students and staff, they afford the students' insufficient time to reflect either on their studies or their practical

97

experience.'[40] The report gives a hint of a further extension to three years, when resources are available. With this we strongly agree.[41] It is not primarily a matter of parity with teachers though the issue has important repercussions there. 'Two years for youth leaders, three years for teachers' gives too easily the impression that it is 'training' for the former and 'education' for the latter, since the extra year makes possible the main and often subsidiary subjects which are ostensibly designed for the personal development of the student. But it is even more a matter of acquiring skill for the job, when that job is recognized as highly skilful, and the whole Service, one hopes, will develop in such a way as to demand more professionals, and more highly-skilled professionals. One college[42] houses both kinds of students— teachers and youth leaders. At the end of three years the first go to their first school where they are junior members of a staff, supported by more experienced colleagues. The second, after two years, may be in charge of a centre with several hundred members, facing, un-supported by immediate professional colleagues, diverse demands.[43] The second require at least as many intellectual resources and oppor-tunities for personal development as the first. Perhaps it is not quite right to describe youth leadership as a profession: yet as Joan Matthews[44] has pointed out, it bears some of the marks of a pro-fession ('he works directly with people according to his own judgment and not according to set prescriptions or in simple response to direct demand'): adequate training is therefore demanded.

Then there is the vexed question of whether full-time youth work can be a life-long career for all those who enter it. The Albemarle Report vainly attempted to solve this dilemma by seeing the teaching profession as being the main source of recruitment when the emergency phase was over. If half the dreams of the new report come true, there will be far more places in which the professional can exercise his skill from school to dance-halls: and within the orthodox boundaries of Youth Service itself there should be expanding opportunities to move into administrative, training or supervisory roles. But this will not meet everybody's need. It ought to be possible for some not only to take a shortened teacher's course—as may happen now—but also a shortened social worker's course, if that is their choice. Much will depend on the content of the training courses. The whole process of transferring to another related job is helped, if there is, as there will be, more inter-professionalism in the training situation. (Though we still wait for the complete training situation where all 'community workers' share a common course in human growth and development, and social studies, and then choose whether they want to be teachers, probation officers, child care officers, community wardens, community relations officers, or youth leaders.) The opportunity to continue part-time education whilst in an appointment is also a related and important factor.

The training courses themselves have to face the demands inherent in the preceding paragraphs. Theoretical and practical aspects of the course must be creatively related. Personal development must find a large place. They must face squarely the dilemma in the question, 'What skills are appropriate to the full-time youth and community worker?' when there are regional variations and impending changes in the Service. (If they move too far ahead of the changing situation, they are not fair to the students since they may be training them for jobs which do not exist; but it would be tragic if the training agencies were out of date.)

At the present time, it is suggested that the answer about skills lies in five areas.

1 *Administrative or managerial* He often has to run an organization.

2 *Group work* He is centrally concerned to help young people to help themselves.

3 *Counselling* Though this word covers different levels of skill and service, yet all will be called upon to give advice to individuals.

4 *Education* He has to stimulate interests and supply and further the interests they have.

5 *Community development* He seeks to relate the work he is doing to the community around and to encourage the discovery and use of the community's own resources.

In a course of at least two years, all can receive training during their first year in all of those basic skills: in the second year, they can specialize in one or even two. Their choice of a specialization may well be related to future training for another role if this is desired.

Finally, true to our signature tune, there are decisions which lie in the hands of full-time leaders themselves. Nobody needs to apologize for them for, having regard to all the circumstances, they have served well. But not all the issues are at the disposal of the 'authorities': an enhanced contribution can come from the professionals by their own efforts, by their courage, integrity, confidence, maturity and—to dare to use a much-maligned word—dedication. If one lists the obvious growing points, it is not to suggest that all, or even the majority of full-time youth workers are deficient in these areas.

1 They could learn to interpret the word 'professional' not in terms of the status or prestige of their job, or their conditions of work—but as applying to the way in which they do their work: 'professional standards' is what is indicated.
2 They could learn to respect what they find even though they are properly full of new ideas: some continuity must be preserved: some of the old foundations are in good condition and can be used for the new structure.
3 They could learn to work in a harmonious and non-servile way with the older people concerned with their job: the youth leader who can 'only get on with young people' is a menace.
4 They could understand that a large part of their duty is the communication of their professional skills to part-timers; of course, 'know-alls' are out, but a full-time worker, though biding his time, knows that he is a 'trainer' of those for whom youth work is only a spare-time occupation.

Notes:

1 *William Smith of the Boys' Brigade*, F. P. Gibbon, Collins, 1934.
2 Percival, op. cit., p. 33.
3 Quoted from Davies & Gibson, op. cit., p. 38.
4 Percival, p. 225.
5 *Eighty Thousand Adolescents*, B. H. Reed, Allen & Unwin, 1950.
6 The argument is developed in the chapter, 'Ideal social conditions for Youth Service'.
7 *New Town Youth, An enquiry into the leisure activities of young people in Peterlee*, The Birmingham Survey, 1969.
   'A round up of local reports', *Youth Review*, November 1968.
   A report on a Survey of Church of England Youth Centres, 1967, C.E.Y.C.
   J. Leighton, *Reaching the Teenager*, Methodist Youth Department, 1966.
8 *Social Education*, Report of a Study Group, Derbyshire Education Committee, 1967, p. 7.
9 Scouts, Advance Party Report, *Design for Scouting*, 1966.
   Boys' Brigade, The Haynes Report, Feb. 1964.
   The Youth Worker and the Young Adult Group, National Association of Youth Clubs, 1969.

C. E. Hartley, 'Guiding in Contemporary Society', *Trends in services for youth*, Pergamon, 1967.
10 Anne Corbett, 'Community School', *New Society*, February 27, 1969.
11 B. Davies and A. Gibson, *The Social Education of the Adolescent*, University of London Press, 1967.
Cyril Smith, *Adolescence*, Longmans, 1968.
J. B. Mays, *The Young Pretenders*, Michael Joseph, 1965.
F. Musgrove, *Youth and the Social Order*, Routledge and Kegan Paul, 1964.
12 *Report of the Committee on the Age of Majority*, H.M.S.O., 1967.
13 In evidence to a committee of the Department of Education and Science.
14 Mary Morse, *The Unattached*, Pelican, 1965.
G. Goestchius and J. Tash, *Working with Unattached Youth*, Routledge and Kegan Paul, 1967.
15 Fred Milson, *Growing with the Job*, National Association of Youth Clubs, 1968.
16 *Girls' Interests*, N.A.Y.C., p. 13.
17 Margaret Mead, *Male and Female*, Pelican, 1962.
18 *Girls in the Nineteen Sixties*, N.A.Y.C., 1963, p. 9.
19 *Social Education*, Derbyshire Education Committee, 1967, p. 8.
20 Alicia Percival, *Youth will be led*, Collins, 1951.
21 B. D. Davies and A. Gibson, *The Social Education of the Adolescent*, University of London Press, 1967, p. 48.
22 J. M. Hogan, *The Relationship between Youth Service and Secondary Schools*, University of Leeds Institute of Education, 1968, p. 13.
23 *The Purpose and Content of the Youth Service*, H.M.S.O., 1945.
24 F. Musgrove, *Youth and the Social Order*, Routledge and Kegan Paul, 1964, pp. 154–5.
25 The two Bessey Reports.
26 *Social Education of Adolescents*, p. 42.
27 P. Halmos, *Faith of the Counsellors*, Constable, 1965.
28 Reported in *New Society*.
29 L. J. Barnes, *Youth Service in an English County*.
30 Fred Milson, Youth Programmes in Jamaica, paper (unpublished) produced by Westhill College of Education.
31 c.f. A. Cohen, *Delinquent Boys*, op. cit.
32 Circular 1486, H.M.S.O., 1939.
33 D. S. Hubery, *Emancipation of Youth*, op. cit., pp. 53–4.
34 G. Ette, *For Youth Alone*, Faber and Faber, 1949.
35 J. M. Brew, *Youth and Youth Groups*, Faber and Faber, 1957, p. 135.
36 *Youth and Community Work in the 70s*, paras. 87–92.
37 *Youth in Contemporary Society, UNESCO Paper*, 1968.
38 Albemarle Report, p. 71.
39 *Youth and Community Work in the 70s*, paras. 230–255.

40   ibid. para. 336.
41   ibid. para. 343.
42   Westhill College of Education, Selly Oak, Birmingham, 29.
43   Derbyshire is one of the few local authorities who so far have produced a scheme which recognizes different levels of responsibility for full-time club leaders.
44   Joan Matthews, *Working with Youth Groups*, University of London Press, 1966, pp. 145f.

5

Guidelines in a new report

Youth and Community Work in the 70s, the recommendations for future policy of the Youth Service Development Council, was issued on October 7th 1969. Mr Edward Short, Secretary of State for Education, writes in the foreword, 'The Government are examining the issues raised by the Report in consultation with many bodies concerned and will announce their conclusions in due course.' In this respect, there is an important difference with the Albemarle Report which included on the front cover the announcement, 'Presented to Parliament by the Minister of Education by Command of Her Majesty February 1960'. The later report may suffer by comparison, seeming to lack authority and support, and be sent out to the public as suggestions rather than accepted government policy. Since it is not offered as 'canonical Scripture', will it be regarded as seriously as Albemarle and have anything like the same effect?

There is at least some advantage in the second approach though admittedly it may give the new report less authority. The intention is that the recommendations will be discussed among many people whom they affect, not least young people themselves. Comments and criticisms have already been invited from many quarters by the Department of Education and Science. They will be considered by the Youth Service Development Council at subsequent meetings and future policy will take serious account of this debate.

That at least is a more democratic process than issuing for action a report which is the work of a small group of people, who have relied upon a number of witnesses, who cannot, with the best intentions, be truly representative of all shades of opinion. And it is more in keeping with a conviction that is growing in our country, that people must not simply be told what to do, but whenever possible, have the opportunity of discussing and influencing decisions which affect their behaviour.

But even more important in this matter, are two facts about Youth Service which make sense of the method of presentation of the new report.

Youth Service in this country relies for maintenance and improvement on persuasion, not edicts. It can argue and seek to challenge and inspire: there are few useful areas in which it can command: it relies for its success upon the willing co-operation of thousands of men and women carrying different responsibilities in the Service. The acceptance of the spirit of the new proposals, and their implementation, depends upon realistic discussion. In general it may be said that people are more likely to put into practice those policies which they themselves have had a share, however small, in formulating.

The second reason which makes sense of the method of presenting the new report is that there are many regional variations in youth work. Different authorities rate its importance differently, if one may judge by the amount of money they are prepared to spend on it: and authorities vary in their emphases and approaches. Many of them appear to have a 'favourite way of doing youth work' either through community colleges or school-based enterprises or some other approaches. There are different patterns of relationships between statutory and voluntary agencies. One area may run many civic centres: another may concentrate on supporting enterprises maintained by voluntary organizations. Yet another variable is the difference between the rural and the urban areas and the undoubted effect this has upon the social experience of young people and the type of approaches which are likely to succeed with them. Hence the difficulty of writing proposals which are equally relevant for every part of the country. And hence the need for local discussions and the feed-back to the Youth Service Development Council.

We may appear to be spending too much time on the presentation of the report, but this is to be defended on the grounds that the report aims to be a plan of action, the outlines of a campaign, not a philosophical treatise on the value of social education. So here, to a marked degree, 'the medium is the message'. A major piece of research waits to be attempted on the fate of government reports. Some are applauded and forgotten: others lead to change. Many factors operate to decide between life in the community for a report, and death on the shelves. One is the presence or absence of a powerful Parliamentary lobby: another is how fortunate the report is in the time of its birth. Does it appear when the issues it raises become matters of public concern because of a related news item? The survival power of a report also relates to the feasibility of its proposals for if they are unrealistic everybody will murmur, 'I quite agree' and promptly dismiss the matter from their minds. But, undoubtedly, one factor is the way in which it is 'sold' to those people who are most concerned with its practical application.

In the present instance, it is significant and to be expected that the popular press settled on the quotable incident of the young man who told the committee that his contemporaries were less concerned with pre-marital sex than with knowing 'how to chat up the birds'. At another level, the report has encountered a mixed reception of approval, disappointment and hostility. Nobody should complain about this. (Temperance reformers have not been pleased by the suggestions that intoxicating drinks should be available in sponsored organizations for the over 18s: a few eyebrows have been raised at the possibility of political education in Youth Service: there are still a few head-masters who think that the school belongs to them and they are not pleased by the proposals for further community use of educational buildings: some of the institutions—like churches, trade unions, indus-try and the commercial entertainment world—may prove to be touchy about the advice offered to them and in one or two cases, the implied criticism.) But what should be acceptable is an insistence that the discussion should centre on the main issues of the report, that is the underlying philosophy, the conclusions and the recommendations. These we hope now to describe and thus turn to the report itself. It is not proposed to reproduce any part of the report in detail, since it is a separate publication, and for those who must run while they read, a summary of the proposals have been provided in a special issue of 'Youth Service' (Volume 9 Number 8), published by the Department of Education and Science.

First, despite what has been said above about the emphasis upon action, the report has an underlying philosophy. As we have several times made plain in the present work, this is right and inevitable, since the question 'What kind of Youth Service do we want in this country?' presupposes that an answer has been attempted to a previous question —'What kind of a society do we want?' We maintain that youth work cannot be effective without a social philosophy. In the present instance, this is expounded in chapter VIII, called 'The Active Society'. People may of course disagree with this platform: they may judge the hopes unattainable and the ideals, woolly. But we make bold to suggest that anybody who finds himself in strong disagreement with the conclusions and recommendations of the report, should read this chapter again and ask himself whether the source of the difference is not a disagreement about the kind of society to be sought. The heart of the argument may be expressed in a brief quotation, 'Our commitment is to a society in which every member can be publicly active. We seek "the active society" in which all are encouraged and enabled to find the public expression of their values, avoiding the extremes of indifference and alienation . . . all individuals should grow towards maturity' (Paragraphs 160, 161 and 164).

The implications of this view are to stress the importance of 'community development', that is, the encouragement at all possible levels of people's involvement in decisions which affect their lives. Running through the report is the belief that community development is a desirable, and to some extent, a possible social goal, and it affects much that is said about Youth Service. Disagreement here is fundamental and will lead to a rejection of specific proposals.

Also in the background lie certain conclusions—sometimes related to evidence received—in respect of the society as a whole and with regard to young people, Youth Service and education in particular. As these are mainly in the issues and dilemmas which have been examined at length in this book, they will be listed here with the repetition of the advice that those who disagree with the recommendations should ask themselves whether this is because they cannot accept the assumptions upon which they are based.

The underlying conclusions are:

1 The age of social adulthood is lower in our society than it was ten years ago. New legislation about the age of majority recognizes a situation that exists: it does not create the situation.

2 The inclusive age-span of 14 to 20 for Youth Service is no longer therefore appropriate, being too wide if the same approaches are made to the older and younger ends.

3 In many respects Youth Service is good but it is not good enough to meet changed conditions: 'there must be a new and imaginative approach'.

4 The 'new' approaches to learning—less didactic and authoritarian, involving the student more actively—are to be encouraged.

5 Youth Service should seek to be more client-centred, starting more frequently than at present from the known needs of young people. This means recognizing priority areas, for example, putting first the needs of those young people who, having left school, find themselves at odds with their society.

6 Youth Service should seek to be related more closely and frequently to the rest of the community. And the acceptance of this rubric will have implications for types of work attempted, joint planning, and approaches to young people themselves.

Finally, turning to the recommendations themselves, we can identify different categories. There are those which may be said to express 'pious hopes', where appeals are made to various partners without specific directions. Perhaps these appeals could not be left out if the picture was to be complete: but they sound banal since they advise a course of action which one would suppose is already accepted. A good example is the counsel offered to voluntary organizations in 9(f): 'National voluntary youth organizations should have close contact with their local branches.' Then there are recommendations which reflect the outlook of the report and which one supposes will be easy to put into effect. A good example here is 6 (a): 'The Youth Service should be redesignated the Youth and Community Service.'
This brings us to the heart of the matter and to those changes which are fundamental and are likely to be most fought-over.

Age-division
Two types of Youth Service are broadly envisaged. The 16s and under should be mainly in the care of the schools and voluntary organizations. (Youth work in schools and colleges should be encouraged.) For the over 16s there should be a more sophisticated provision which recognizes the adulthood of young people, with large elements of self-determination. The change-over from one type to the other should not be rigidly enforced, but largely left to personal choice. 2(c), (d), 6(c)

A community-based Youth Service
Youth work must be seen to be happening, and be encouraged, at many places in our society and not just inside youth organizations. And it must help young people to relate to their community, to act responsibly and to think for themselves. 2(a), (f), 6(a), (o), 7(d), 8(m)

A client-centred Youth Service
Attempts must be made to understand the real and varied needs of young people and to meet the particular needs of certain social groups —the handicapped, the 'immigrants', the anti-social and so on. Priority

for grants should go to schemes to help those who have left school, have a poor social environment and have special difficulty in finding their place in society. Priority is also to be given to mixed club work— since one of the objects is 'to bring young adults of both sexes together', and to organizations which 'help young people to create and find their place in society'. 1, 2(a), (f), 5(d), 6(p), 7(c)

Comprehensive planning for social education
A number of clauses are concerned with this aim and they are directed to different quarters—government departments, local authorities and voluntary organizations: they call for common policies wherever possible, the joint use of resources, physical and human, and the avoidance of overlapping, waste, fragmentation of effort and insularity. 2(g), 5(g), (h), (j), 7(e), 8(d-j), 9(h, c, f)

Publicity
'The existing Youth Service has suffered from a poor image.' To remedy this, there is a demand for a clear policy statement from the Secretary of State, and the use, nationally, of the most modern and effective means of publicity. 6(e, f)

Administration
The report believes that administrative changes, particularly at the local government level, would help forward the process of community development, which, as they centrally affirm, will both help and be helped by an adequate Youth Service. 'We urge local authorities to consider whether their procedures facilitate participation in community service and allow a response to changing situations. Where they do not, they ought to be reorganized.' Elsewhere, on the same subject, they consider it better for the Service to remain within the Department of Education and Science who should be responsible for setting the pace and bringing other government departments together for relevant action for young people. 1(g), 7(a), 8(b)

Partnership
'The new Youth and Community Service will bring exciting possibilities for new partnerships between the Service and industry, trade unions, the commercial enterprises, the social services and education.' The report may be said to begin this process by presuming to offer advice to various institutions concerned with young people. Churches

are to look at the use of their premises, the training of clergy and their role in the light of the demand for community. (It has already been said by one commentator that it is a long time since the Government offered advice to the Church.) Trade Unions are invited to involve young people more in decision-making: industry and commerce to link with youth and community work; and managers of coffee bars and dance halls to do the same. (1g, 11c, b, 12 a, b, c)

Full-time youth and community workers

The report recognizes that there are vital implications in the new policy for the recruitment, training, deployment and status of full-time workers in the new Service. Only better pay and prospects will attract people of the right calibre. Training courses are to be of two-years' duration from September 1970, with a possibility of three years when economic conditions permit. The content of the course must take account of the need for the worker to be involved with youth in the community, and not just in the youth organization. Special attention should be devoted to counselling skills, but as there are many aspects of the role, there should be an opportunity to specialize in one or two of the skills. Inter-professional links with other educationists and social workers must be encouraged at every level: and opportunities provided to transfer to other related roles, with further training, after a period in youth and community work. 2(h), 6(k, l), 7(f), 8(n), 10(a-d), 13

As we have repeatedly observed, there is no panacea for youth work in this country, but the authors of this report believe that they have pointed in the right direction towards an up-to-date, adequate and relevant service. On this, at present, they wait for their work to be judged.

6

Distant goals and paths towards them

President Kennedy liked to think of himself as an 'idealist without illusions': he wanted to be seen as a leader who never lost sight of ultimate goals but who spent his time searching for the immediate paths: thus he defended himself against the opposing criticisms that he was unprincipled or starry-eyed. Whatever the political value of this position, pragmatic idealism is the best hope for an improvement in British Youth Service.

Statements about ideal goals in the Service are likely to rouse opposition from two sources. There are, first, hard-pressed practitioners burdened with the day-to-day running of an organization who find those theories an annoying irrelevance. A beautiful theory is not always attractive to a youth worker who is struggling with problems of discipline in a rough area, whose club is receiving regular visits from teenage gangs intent on trouble: who has to spend a fair amount of time on bread and butter problems like getting in the subscriptions, paying the bills, maintaining the grant: who is also troubled by periodic quarrels among some of his adult helpers. In such circumstances, any advice from outside sources should be offered in tactful terms. Yet long acquaintance, at many levels, with youth work, emboldens us to say that there is another side. On enquiry it is often found that overworked leaders are people who cannot or will not delegate real authority to others: they must have all the bigger strings in their own hands: either because they suspect that nobody in the organization is as efficient as they are ('If you want a job done well, do it yourself'), or they are not secure enough to share authority ('There can only be one leader in this club'). More than this, it is a severely practical matter for a youth worker to lift his head from his task from time to time, and ask himself and his colleagues what is the object of the exercise: to become bogged down with the daily details is to run the risk of being busy without a sense of direction. Many

110

youth workers are happy to admit that they need to get away from the youth organization for a while to see it in proper perspective, just as G. K. Chesterton, who lived in Battersea, once said he was going on a world tour to see Battersea in true focus. Statements of goals have meaning for busy youth workers.

Criticism is likely to come from a different quarter. Academic psychologists and sociologists often question whether there can be a statement of aims since we lack the necessary research material for the exercise. Since any philosophy of youth work is likely to be fashioned from the value-judgments and prejudices of older people, it will probably reflect middle-class standards. Many of the phrases which are dear to the hearts of youth work enthusiasts encounter a sceptical reception from sociologists. No doubt these phrases are often used thoughtlessly: once they begin to be used everybody wants to be on the bandwaggon and begins to use them: no one wants to deny that youth work philosophies and approaches need to be repeatedly chastened by the findings of reliable research. But our answer to the academics is the opposite of our justification to the practitioners. Youth work is a practical affair: it must be carried on using the best knowledge that we have at the moment: we must act before we know everything. Sociologists may be able to afford to be non-judgmental, to hesitate to make pronouncements until there is more light, to wait for the results of long and costly research projects: but youth workers cannot be so relaxed. They are involved in the human situation with young people now and they have to make decisions that some aims and methods are better than others.

One example of the gulf between youth worker and sociologist fits our theme. A broad definition of an overall purpose for the service today is that it seeks the social education of the young. As we have seen, this makes sense historically, since the efforts are no longer directed to providing basic education, or meeting economic needs or being primarily a means of Christian education and evangelism—all of which were dominant themes at various stages in the development of youth movements. What is left? Young people are growing up in a complex society. They are presented, as J. B. Mays has pointed out, with a bewildering number of choices. 'The world at this stage of the youngsters' development looks more like a gigantic cafeteria or vast emporium more than anything else.'[1] In growing areas of personal life there is less effective guidance from society as to what one may hope for and how one is expected to behave. Various formulae have been used to describe the adolescent task in a society like ours. Mays says it is adjustment to self—the discovery of identity —adjustment to society—the acceptance of a new status among one's fellows—and adjustment to the world—the working out of one's own philosophy, one's own interpretation of the mystery of human existence. Elsewhere, it has been said that adolescence is a valley of decision where four major decisions are normally made—whom to marry, what job to do, what self-image to hold and what personal philosophy. The rationale of Youth Service is that if a modern society cannot always provide the means for the accomplishment of these adolescent tasks, then peer-groups may help. Here the youngster can meet with others passing through the same stage: together they may learn and experiment with life: together they may discover their own personal and social identity, and their own individual possibilities. The youth group can be a buffer state between the protected world of childhood and the exposed world of the adult. And there is always the hope that a suitable adult will be around to give counselling, educational and organizational help if required.

This is what is meant by saying that the primary motive of Youth Service in a society like ours is 'social education'. (Of course, there are additional by-products, like sometimes finding useful and satisfying activity for adults whose lives might otherwise be empty and boring. But it is the primary goal which justifies the effort and the expense. The primary goal of a hospital is to cure illness and ease pain: a delightful and important by-product is that doctors may fall in love with nurses: but the expense of a hospital could not be justified by the incidence of romances among staff. And success or failure in reaching the primary goal is the criterion for achievement in any enterprise. A football team does not usually say, 'We lost every match we played last season, but we had some good times together.')

But 'social education' is a phrase likely to be sniffed at in intellectual circles where it may be said that we simply do not know what it means: and of course we do not know perfectly: we often use the phrase carelessly and we should constantly examine our use of it and ask ourselves what we mean: and moreover, in a changing society like ours, it becomes increasingly difficult to define the boundaries of the subject. Nevertheless, our argument is that the youth worker is compelled to make practical decisions: no doubt he will make even better decisions when his academic colleagues have provided him with more accurate information: but against that day he cannot suspend operations: he is involved with young people and though perhaps he could not write a paper on the subject, yet he recognizes areas of achievement and possibilities in the social education of the members. As he thinks about the youth group with which he is working, the following points may emerge.

1   Members vary according to the degree of their social and emotional maturity. At one end of the scale are those who can think of others, project themselves into the experience of others, realize the effect of their own actions upon others, co-operate with others, give a lead when that is required and follow a lead when that is appropriate. At the other end of the scale are those who do not seem to have moved far from the egocentricity of babyhood: they see the world and events too exclusively in terms of self: perhaps they remind the worker of the patients whom Peer Gynt met.

> *Sailing with outspread sails of self.*
> *Each shuts himself in a cask of self,*
> *The casket stopped with a bung of self*
> *And seasoned in a well of self.*
> *None has a tear for others' woes*
> *Or cares what any other thinks.*

2   The social and emotional maturity or immaturity of the youngsters is usually related to the homes in which they have grown up. Families where the youngsters have not felt loved or families where they have found indulgence rather than affection, tend to produce unstable insecure or spoilt—and therefore immature—youngsters. Families where they have met firm affection and experienced an ethos of caring even for folk outside the family, produce mature youngsters who can co-operate, discriminate and develop stable relationships.

3   He is not waiting for any survey to tell him—as a rough and ready judgment(!)—that maturity is 'better' than immaturity. Apart from any ethical considerations, people who are aware of the needs and feelings of others are likely to have on the whole interesting and satisfying lives and they will certainly cause less unhappiness to their fellows.

4   Experience in a youth group can often contribute to the social and emotional development of the youngster at a decisive stage of

his personal growth. Here he may learn once more that you cannot always have what you want at the precise moment when you want it: that it is often necessary to support a majority decision that you don't like: that if you want to be acceptable to other people, you have to learn how to please them: that much happiness is only possible through co-operation and teamwork.

5   Thus in the youth group, the adolescent may begin to learn how to make that variety of personal relationships which are 'the best portion of a good man's life'. There is the well-known division according to authority. Can you get on reasonably well with the boss, your mates and your subordinates, that is with those above you, alongside you and beneath you? There are, for example, many adults who cannot be on easy terms with anybody who has authority over them—they must be servile or aggressive. (The headmaster of a public school used to recount with glee an incident when he thought he was succeeding. One night he was playing cards with three of his prefects. He trumped the ace of the boy sitting next to him: the boy looked up and remarked pleasantly, 'You swine, *sir*.') But this simple division does little justice to the variety of personal relationships which we are called upon to make in our lives—as children, parents, friends, husbands or wives—each with their own expectations and patterns. The vast majority of young people will not be social analysts or political revolutionaries, but they will make friends, fall in love, marry and have children.

6   But social education in the youth group need not be confined to learning how to make different types of personal relationships, decisive as this skill often proves to be for the individual. It can also relate to, for example, the ability to make personal choices about entertainment, dress styles and attitudes. It has become fashionable to talk about the 'emancipation of youth': but at most they are only half free like those coloured folk in the Deep South. Or if it is true that they have hitherto been enslaved by the adult members of the community—as certain writers strive to convince us—they have merely exchanged the old tyrant for a new one—about which those same writers have little to say. For too often the young people in this country are at the mercy of commercial interests who have put two facts together and come up with an insidious advertising campaign. The first fact is the undoubted emotionality of young people and com-

merce often sets out to supply goods and services to meet this need: the other is the undoubted affluence of young people, more emphatic because they are at a stage of little financial responsibility: hence the scramble to create 'brand loyalty' and the exploitation of drives for which there is not for the young, a socially-acceptable outlet. Far from being 'free men' the young are often simply 'propaganda suckers'. Youth workers will do little to change the tone of advertising: they will not tear the elaborate network of lies which has been thrown around all our shoulders: they will not chase the unconvinced communicators from our television screens nor end the sickening chorus and the false heartiness of the salesmen who want to be our friends. But at the other end, a youth group is a place where teenagers may look more sceptically at the goods and services which are offered to them so persuasively.

7   Social education is concerned also to help young people to be discriminating about their society. R. K. Merton[2] has drawn the distinction between the destructive revolutionary who wants to contract out of society as retreatist or anarchist: and the constructive revolutionary who wants to work for radical changes which will improve society. It has been a defect about much recent discussion, that observers have often appeared to conclude that a young person must either be a beatnik—'Stop, the world I want to get off'—or a neatnik—'How can I get on in this kind of world?' A third species is possible—the young person who is learning what to accept and what to reject in the society in which he finds himself. That this is not nearly so theoretical as it may sound can be shown by two illustrations. In one of our largest cities, there is a Youth Parliament, whose young representatives, elected by young people, meet to discuss the current civic issues and occasionally organize peaceful political action. The second illustration arises from the experience of at least a few young people in voluntary work for the community: not all of them have been content only to give personal service and give no thought to the values of a society which allows these conditions to arise: not all have visited old ladies in inadequate accommodation and asked no questions about welfare and housing policies. The pity is not that a vociferous protest against society comes from a minority of the younger generation: the pity is that so often that protest is emotional rather than political, ludicrously inadequate in ideas for feasible reform. Some youth leaders at least have demonstrated that social

education programmes can guide youthful idealism into positive and constructive and not necessarily, less radical forms.

We are arguing then that to define the goal has meaning despite possible protests from practitioners and theoreticians. At least it gives us an idea of the direction in which to move, and if we only inch forward slowly, it helps us to resemble pilgrims and explorers, rather than tourists and wanderers. A few years ago, Mr Roy Jenkins, when Home Secretary, defined the goal of a multi-racial society as containing the three elements of equal opportunity, cultural diversity and mutual tolerance. Nobody supposes the situation in say, Bradford, Birmingham or Wolverhampton meets this threefold demand; but if we can agree on the definition, at least it gives us something to aim at and a measuring rod: even if we do not agree, at least it provides a clear statement to argue about. The statement of a distant goal can encourage, not discourage us, unless we insist on being depressed by the disparity between vision and achievement.

AN IDEAL YOUTH SERVICE

All over the world, in modern, industrial, urban and democratic societies there is what is called 'a youth problem': they talk about it in London, California, West Berlin and Hong Kong. We may suspect that it does not feature so prominently in Communist countries (where, for example, is the students' revolt in East Germany?) mainly because the thoughts and acts of young people in totalitarian countries are more rigidly controlled by the authorities. In the Western world, we are familiar with aspects of alienation of a section of the youth population from the rest of their community. The features vary but prominent are drug-addiction, rejection of adult norms of behaviour, generational tension, and an increase of juvenile crime, particularly violent crime.

Of course this deviant behaviour is characteristic only of a minority of the youth population anywhere (though it has recently been reported that there are 10 million on 'soft' drugs in the U.S.A.). But we must beware of the fallacy of minimizing human problems by reducing them to percentages. To say that ·004% of the students in X University took their own lives during the last academic year is less startling than reporting that 20 undergraduates committed suicide. A racialist will be less disturbed by the statement that under 2% of Britain's population is coloured than being told there are nearly one million coloured people in these islands. Statistics also suffer from the defect of adding together things which are not the same as for example in juvenile delinquency returns where the boy who has raided an orchard is counted alongside the boy who has derailed a locomotive or set fire to a church.

There is cause for concern in the 'youth problem' for those who think that 'Western' democratic societies are not wholly bad, that a moral tradition which has taken centuries to form should not lightly and wholly be cast aside, that there is a 'national identity' which has to be passed on to the new generation who must acquire habits of social responsibility and learn their duties as well as their rights. And curiously enough, the fact that most adult people think in roughly the way that has been described in the last sentence, contributes a threat to Youth Service. For it means that most people will think of it as a device for 'knocking some sense into the young people' and as an immediate panacea for the ills which come to a society through the 'revolt of youth'. The second hope is likely to be disappointed since most of the 'results' of youth work are long term and it rarely transforms any scene quickly. For example, even an ideal Youth Service would not quickly reduce the incidence of drug-addiction or violent crime among the young. It could properly insist on more clinics for the first and say, a better equipped probation service for the latter. In the end, by meeting the boredom and aimlessness and lack of social significance of young people, it could reduce both the amount of drug-taking and juvenile crime. But the objection to the first expectation is more serious. An ideal Youth Service would spring as much from hope and confidence and pride in young people as it would from fear: a Youth Service which makes an undue reliance upon fear will weaken its influence with young people.

Much of what is written in this present volume is a plea against the frequent insularity of Youth Service: 'You in your small corner and I in mine' would be a suitable description of many enterprises: and this insularity is to be found at different levels. Nationally, it operates when there is insufficient consultation between different government departments concerned with the welfare of the young. It can be found sometimes in voluntary organizations and among local youth workers. We are often bedevilled by those human failings which make us confuse smaller with greater loyalties—anxiety, possessiveness, the bureaucratic mind. An ideal Youth Service would come out of its frequent isolation and would be happy to live on a large map.

It would be content to give hospitality to the notion that the social education of the young people could better be undertaken by other agencies—like schools, spontaneous youth groups, dance halls—though as I have said, it seems to me that at the moment, youth can best be served by retaining a separate identity for Youth Service along with the growing other provisions. But like other institutions, Youth Service should be ready to die in order to live. Important as is the matter of the status of the professionals, it should never be allowed to obscure the real purpose of the exercise. And we should be eager to recognize the realms from which we have much to receive as well as to give—education both secondary and further, social work, social reform, political action and community development. We should rejoice if the best approaches and intentions of youth work spill over into the community and thereby lower the levels in youth organizations.

Those who have the courage and generosity and confidence to put first the needs of young people are not likely to find themselves unused and unwanted. This brings us to the first standard of a potent Youth Service: it would be client-centred, existing always for the sake of the young people themselves. First consideration is given to the personal development of the young people, and decisions are guided by the priority accorded to this factor.

An early effect of taking seriously this standard, would be that Youth Service would show more flexibility than at present and we should break away from the familiar stereotyped forms—clubs and uniformed organizations. It would mean immediately that 'Youth Service' would be found in far more places since it would simply be a generic term indicating the social education for those who have ceased to be children but are not yet, in the full sense, emotional and social adults. Moreover, within youth organizations themselves, the rubric would lead to more varied programmes, since there are many different needs in a youth group and a varied programme reflects the desire to meet those needs rather than to have an impressive organization which looks good on paper and to the official visitor. A client-orientated service would take account of the differences and similarities of the clients—girls, the handicapped, the coloured teenagers and those in need of counselling. It looks an odd collection but they belong to each other because they have special needs (even the girls in a Service run mainly for boys); yet they should not always be marked off from the others. When the 'Hunt' Committee was pursuing

118

its enquiries about the educational experience of coloured teenagers, they were met by several authorities who said, 'We have no problem: we do not distinguish between black and white youngsters.' This sounds good but it may mean that the special needs of coloured youngsters were not being met. Those authorities had not heard of the Plowden argument that if you give the same to each, some may be deprived because of their greater need. (A stringent test of any educational-social work provision is whether it can take account both of similarities and differences among those whom it seeks to serve.) Such a Service will labour to find out whether any contribution can be made to the challenges which arise in various areas of the young-ster's experiences (and not be content merely to seek a 'good club member')—at work—at home—in possibilities for further education both liberal and vocational—in the love-courtship-marriage sequence. Not least it will make nice and careful calculations on the 'permission and support' balance. And it will know and act upon its knowledge, as to how far youngsters need to be left alone to work out their own problems and how far they need help.

Equally an ideal Youth Service will be community-based and this again is a standard with several parts. It will not want to hang on to youngsters—to keep up the numbers or not to lose a helpful person—when they are at the stage when they should normally be moving out into the wider community: indeed, it will constantly be building bridges for the members from the youth organizations into the community, advertising courses at the college of further education on the club notice board and so on. It will not mourn the loss of a member who decides say to spend his evening at the local political club of his choice, for it recognizes that though youth movements are properly concerned to provide fun, yet they have a serious purpose too. They want to release into our society mature adults who can carry responsibility, who will neither accept unthinkingly, nor reject contemptuously, what they find there: adequate citizens for a time of change: able to make a contribution to a community whose watch-words, we have suggested, should be compassion and participation.

At the present time there are signs—little as a human hand—of a growing generational tension: indeed there are indications of a mounting adult backlash against students' revolts and hippies' activities, after the first indulgent tolerance which greeted the appearance of this reality. (A common habit is to contrast the calm efficiency of the police with the hysterical exaggerations of the young revolutionaries.) Wrote

Mr Quintin Hogg in the *Sunday Express* (September 28th 1969): 'Between the television programme of the moonshot men or the tumultuous welcome accorded to Sir Francis Chichester and the pictures of the arrogant, ignorant, untrained, feckless and plain dirty squatters evicted from Piccadilly and Endell Street there could hardly be a greater contrast. They might be the inhabitants of different planets. It seems incredible that they belong to the same species of *homo sapiens.*'

When human beings quarrel they often begin to fix devil's horns to the heads of their opponents. But an ideal Youth Service would be an active agent—perhaps the most active agent—for reconciliation and understanding between the older and younger members of our community. It would not be concerned merely to damp down the conflict. Even more it would use it as a learning experience for both sides. This too is what is meant by saying that an ideal Youth Service would be community-based.

IDEAL SOCIAL CONDITIONS FOR YOUTH SERVICE

Nobody can look carefully at youth movements without finding himself asking questions about our society; Youth Service is a window through which he is, in the end, viewing the whole of our life together in Britain. (We have previously noted the fact that many of the earlier pioneers became social reformers.) For Youth Service cannot exist in a vacuum; its possibilities and opportunities are conditioned by what is happening in the society as a whole. The work is more likely to flourish in a certain environment and in this section we ask ourselves what the ideal conditions would be and what are the changes that would be most decisive.

Though it sounds like crying for the moon, the first demand is for a change in public opinion about the young, for a profound difference that is in the way adults think about the younger generation. As we have seen, they are today often viewed as a threat. (A few years ago in Dorset a group of teenagers were advancing on an old folks' home with axes in their hands. A woman who saw this terrifying spectacle went into a telephone booth and dialled the emergency number for the police. With impressive efficiency, a police car arrived at the old folks' home in a few minutes, to find the teenagers chopping firewood for the old people, which had been their intention from the beginning.) Sometimes they are regarded with awe as the heralds of a new way of life that none of the rest of us have had the courage to adopt; they have embraced freedom and permissiveness and dare to live 'for the kicks'. Or they are seen to be there to be exploited either because we older people want to make a profit by selling to them our goods—cosmetics, cigarettes, food, clothes, records, films— or because we want to persuade them to join a movement in which we older people have invested our lives and we know the movement can only live by drawing recruits from the rising generation. The movement can be religious, political or relate to a special interest. How often one hears the lament from veterans of traditional organizations, 'I am afraid the young people do not seem interested.'

In a civilized community, the most frequent message flashed across the generations from older to younger people would be 'Come over and help us.' The young are best seen as social partners with the old, called to share a destiny in the last decades of the twentieth century but a destiny which is not yet clear. So the young are invited on equal terms to define the task as well as to share its labours; we need their ideas as well as their muscles or their willingness to put circulars in envelopes; they should be active not sleeping partners. There is ample evidence that this approach finds an encouraging response from a significant number of young people and often in unexpected quarters. There is nothing so encouraging as a cry for help. And the failure of many of our institutions—for example, churches, trade unions and political parties—to flash this message has more to do than we think with the 'youth problem'. A public which entertained these hopes would rejoice to discover all those places where the partnership was working and they would be far more likely to support a Youth Service which would be seen as one organized expression of the intention.

There is one further aspect of common public attitudes to the young. One wishes that more people could learn to discriminate between what to applaud and accept and what to criticize in the behaviour of teenagers. At present, there is too often a straightforward acceptance or a straightforward rejection. To criticize them for their hair or dress styles or preferences in music, theatre or art, is ridiculous; these are matters of taste. Does that mean we must never criticize them and abdicate from any position of responsibility? If we find them lacking in ideals and chivalry and tendresse, taking their pleasure where they find it without thought of the consequences for others, emphatic about their rights but silent about their duties—then respectful controversy should begin. For most people these are not neutral matters where opinions are not important. Life has pronounced against selfishness; the film *Alfie* shows that in the end he is without friends. If there has to be a battle between older and younger members in the community, the older section should choose the ground carefully.

The efforts of the Youth Service would further be strengthened if there was a widespread appreciation of the value of social education. One is far more likely to find this in official documents and in annual conferences than in the conversations in a pub or a launderette. The issue is simply that education is for personal development as a human being, not for acquiring information, passing examinations, gaining qualifications and enhanced prestige in our society: it is for living as well as for making a living: education should be for fellowship, not a contribution to the rat race. Yet most of us have observed that education is the surest road to a better job and enhanced prestige in our society: there is widespread support for an elitist view of education as the search for and encouragement of talent ('train the best, and shoot the rest'). An enthusiasm for social education reaches back to a belief that it is important to be a human being whether you 'get on' or not. But this is not a widely-held conviction. How often does one hear a parent say, 'That school was very good for Johnny even though he did not gain any C.S.Es'? And so long as the social and human aspects of education are undersold in this country, Youth Service will not receive the public support it requires for it is in business primarily to provide social education. One constantly hears of 'immigrant' parents who do not encourage their children to go to youth organizations—perhaps understandably—on the grounds that 'there is no qualification at the end'.

We have been thinking of society as a whole and public opinion in general: but under ideal conditions for Youth Service there would be changes in the outlook and practices of various institutions.

One thinks first of all of the educational institutions and in particular of those officials who both at national and local level, plan our educational provision. They are a much-maligned race partly because they are an obvious scapegoat when things go wrong. But they usually prove on closer knowledge to be devoted people with high professional standards, or, as councillors, men anxious to do the right thing. Perhaps the professionals are a little inclined to know what is good for the customer without bothering to find out what the customer thinks.

My own experience over the last ten years has been that there is more progressive and radical thinking about education among the professional educationalists, particularly inspectors, than among any other section of the population.

What most of all bedevils the system and has a particularly baleful effect upon Youth Service, is the fragmentation of the structure. People become involved in one section of the field—they are soon acting as though that is the whole field. (They are faintly reminiscent of a group of three hundred Eskimos living in the vicinity of Smith Sound, in the north of Greenland. Weyer says that a few decades ago these Eskimos believed themselves to be the only inhabitants of the universe. They had been isolated from other groups of Eskimos for some generations and knew of no other men except by legend.)[3] Youth Service suffers first and most severely by this fragmentation. Under pressure for economies recently, a Northern authority simply abolished its total training scheme for part-time youth workers. Comprehensive planning sees the picture as an integrated whole and does not undervalue social education. Youth Service would gain enormously by this practice.

The Churches, of course, have a distinguished record in youth work and they continue to be one of the major partners. But one wonders whether they have thought out their role in a society which is becoming increasingly secular in the sense that more and more decisions are taken nationally and locally, without reference to Divine Law. Do they see themselves as primarily 'gathered communities', a large Ark in which the faithful are to be housed during the turbulent storms of the twentieth century? Or do they see themselves as the agents of a leaven to be spread throughout the land, influencing people, being an effective part of the humanizing process in Britain, but not expecting many people (except the few guardians of the faith that was once for all delivered to the saints) to make a personal commitment to the faith? To be fair, the different demonminations might give different answers to this question. On the whole, a clear answer has been given by the national leaders of the churches. They make the second choice: they frequently refer to 'the Christian's involvement with the secular': they want to go into business with community development as an offer. But in practice this is not a view which is shared by most members of most congregations: *they* see the church as a place of renewal and association for the convinced. Many an incumbent today is agonizing to persuade the majority of his lay people to take larger views: in many churches and chapels, youth leaders seek to help the youngsters of the neighbourhood whilst some of the faithful complain that the work has little value because few of the club members come to church: ambitious schemes for youth work in churches have sometimes broken down because the unspoken expectations of larger congregations have not been fulfilled. (In one case, where many youngsters from a poor district were being attracted into a church youth club, a church official complained to the minister, 'You are bringing the wrong type of young person on to these premises.') Local churches which had unequivocally entered the business of community development would make a major contribution to youth work throughout the land.

Trade unions and political parties are also interested in young people and they have strong motivations, since only recruits from another generation can ensure the persistence of the movements. The trade unions, at least the larger ones, have impressive educational pro- grammes—at least they are impressive on paper. But my experience of their practice—limited it is true—is that they are not nearly so impressive there. I know of many young workers for whom the union is only an organization to which weekly dues are paid under pressure from older workers. Of the history of the trade union movement, of its present struggle to find a role in English society, as distinct from the task of getting more money and better conditions for members, they know nothing. In recruiting young members, the political parties face the widespread political apathy of the young and their disillusionment with all political parties: too often the conflicts look like the quarrels of an older generation. In both areas I have found—though not univer- sally—examples of entrenched old-fashioned attitudes to the young. They are there to receive a tradition: to be impressed by the longer experiences and riper wisdom of the older people: 'theirs not to reason why'. If the ideas of young people were treated more seriously in trade unions or political parties, if their critical participation was welcomed, the work of the youth movements would benefit for it would link with the purpose of active involvement in society. Two cautionary tales illustrate the point. In the 1964 General Election, a youth leader of a large club invited each of the three candidates in the local con- stituency to visit the club and put their case. No reply was received from any of the three. There were no votes at the time for the under 21s. By contrast, the writer was once the leader of a youth club where the local M.P. was a member of the Cabinet. In response to my invitation, he came for Sunday tea whenever he was in the constituency and tried to explain the political issues to the club members. Perhaps there was a political gain but those youngsters felt they were being taken seriously by a politician.

Finally, Youth Service could benefit by a change of attitude to young people in industry. There are of course many industrialists who give large support to youth work both in and off their premises. Moreover, one recognizes that industry is mainly concerned to make a profit. But it is disappointing to find that in commenting on the young, industrialists are prone to approve of those purposes which are obviously and directly related to higher production—self-discipline, purpose and control. That is why it is commoner to find industrialists supporting boys' club work than mixed club work, approving of masculine activities rather than better personal relationships. An appreciation by industry of the human and social purposes of Youth Service would be valuable: and it might not be altogether irrelevant for production, since on the whole, happy people, who are not bored or frustrated, will work harder.

IMMEDIATE STEPS

It could properly be objected at this point that if we had a society remotely resembling the description of the last section, there would be no need for an elaborate and costly Youth Service; there would be many places at which the young were receiving social education and separate organizations would be unnecessary. This is probably true: but our society, and no other in the modern world so far as we know, fits the description. Therefore those who work in Youth Service should ask themselves two questions. How can we be as effective as the social conditions will allow? What kind of Youth Service will contribute to a society which encouraged the education of the young?

There is no panacea that will make Youth Service client-related and community-based, partly because as we have seen much of the effort and improvement is not mandatory. Progress depends upon the willing co-operation of a host of responsible people with varying kinds and degrees of responsibility. The Service is voluntary in more than the simple sense that young people may accept or reject the offer: success or failure is decided by many adults who work within it, full-time, part-time paid or voluntary. A national policy may plead and persuade: it cannot command.

The big regional differences in the position and pattern of Youth Service—how seriously it is treated, the balance of effort between statutory and voluntary effort, the particular emphasis on different approaches like school-based work and related matters—make it difficult to offer practical suggestions which are everywhere equally applicable: in this matter, meat for one area may be poison for another. (The point has been explored in the chapter on the new report.)

With these limitations in mind, it is possible to make a few suggestions in the belief that they are of fairly wide application. They are offered within a framework which has been described in the preceding paper.

1 Improvements are most likely to come through frank and open discussions between all the parties concerned.

2 Improvement is measured by how far we move in the direction of a client-related and community-based provision as these terms have been defined in the previous section.

3 Towards this end we have suggested three areas of improvement:

a Comprehensive planning for social education and an end of wasteful fragmentation of effort.

b Securing a more informed public support for the Service that will lead to wider and deeper involvement.

c Raising the skills of all those who work directly with young people: these skills may variously be educational, counselling and organizing.

First then, we suggest that every local education authority sponsor a conference to consider the new report in general, and in particular three questions.

1 'What are the gaps in the provision for the social education of young people in this area? Is it the older teenagers? or girls? or "immigrant" youngsters? or the handicapped? or the anti-social?'

2 'How can we plan the joint use of our resources of money, premises and manpower to help the social development of young people in our area?'

3 'What means are we using to make known to the general public the purpose of youth work and hence to gain further support and new recruits for the work?' This gathering should be truly representative. (This is not impossible: similar gatherings were called throughout the land after the issue of the second Bessey Report.) It should certainly include representatives of the young people themselves, of the

voluntary organizations, of social agencies like the Probation Service, Child Care and the Youth Employment Service, as well as councillors and local government officials representing education both for schools and further education. Of course, such a meeting will be large and unwieldy: it could easily end in just one more talking session with the airing of pious hopes. It must organize itself into working parties committed to the exploration of specific areas with recommendations for action: the areas of interest will come from the conference but they might well include purpose and aims, training, barriers to co-operation, new methods and approaches, and publicity. The working parties would meet regularly—say once a month through three months—but would have a strictly limited life. If all this sounds impractical, let me say that I personally know many youth workers, in different parts of the country, at present frustrated and disappointed, who eagerly wait for such a consultation and confrontation.

As we have seen, there are vast regional differences, but from my sketchy knowledge of different areas, I would expect a number of discoveries to be made fairly frequently. One is that nobody has the responsibility for the 'public relations' job in Youth Service as a whole, as distinct from being responsible for the publicity of a particular organization which requires financial support from the public. This item should be on the agenda of every authority and Youth Committee: and there should be one person who includes among his duties the responsibility of seeing that the public is kept informed of the intentions of Youth Service and the importance of social education. Then I would expect that in most areas gaps would in fact be found, youngsters who are not receiving the service which is appropriate to their needs. Usually when committees come together to review the work, they congratulate themselves on what is being done. They applaud the figures of young people who attend the community college or the school-based club: they rarely stop to ask about those youngsters who will not be attracted by this type of provision, simply because there is no one type of provision which will prove attractive to all: the real test of an authority's youth policy is its variety and flexibility. Even when areas of unprovided need are identified, it will not always mean that they can all be met immediately, but even to identify them is a step in the right direction: and some gaps in many places could be filled by the joint use of resources. Next, I would expect a radical appraisal of the total situation frequently to lead to discoveries about part-time leaders—their recruitment, training

F

and deployment. For example, it is not unknown for an authority to rely upon newspaper announcements to gather part-time workers whereas experience has shown that some more personal approach is likely to succeed, both in gaining more recruits and recruits with more to offer. One large authority which tried both approaches in a recruiting campaign—the impersonal and the personal—found that almost without exception the recruits had responded to the second kind of invitation. Nor need this mean that we are simply relying upon present youth workers to bring their friends (though as a source of recruitment this is not to be despised): in the particular case just referred to, principals in every college of further education visited each class and explained the opportunity to students. (Incidentally, there is another practical step which may properly be mentioned here. Many opportunities are being lost by the failure to offer community development, as a subject and as a skill, on the curriculum of colleges of further education. This would have a wide application. And why should we assume that youth workers can only be trained in a group marked 'Youth workers in training'?) Finally, I would expect that any honest assessment would find that there were areas of overlapping, where different branches of the same 'business' are competing for the same 'customers'. Is there co-ordination of effort not only at national and authority levels, but at district? Are training programmes co-ordinated wherever possible? Do voluntary organizations have to be 'general providers' or could they specialize in a needy field? Is there overlapping of staff? The urgency of these questions is that resources must be released to meet the many demands we have to face.

Turning from the hopes which arise for action and improvement from local consultations, there is a suggestion for a contribution to the whole field of social education from colleges of education. We have already seen that optional youth courses for teachers have become popular: there is general agreement that the scheme has been successful, not only in providing youth tutors, but in raising the general teaching skills of those who have taken part in those courses. But why should the opportunity of working with a voluntary youth group, using the skills of informal education, be restricted to those who take on this additional work? Why should it not be part of the course for all those who are preparing themselves to be secondary school teachers and be counted as part of 'teaching practice'. Most departments of education in the colleges today would be unhappy with a division which saw class work as only formal education and youth work the only possibility of informal education for young people. But Area Training Organizations differ in their willingness to accept this arrangement and certainly some of them seem to be working with a stereotyped picture of education as being formal (and classroom) education. The acceptance of work in a youth group, as part of the preparation for all secondary school teachers in training, could pay a large bonus in schools, school-based Youth Service, in youth organizations and in inter-professional understanding between teachers and youth leaders.

It has, however, been made clear that, in the view of the present writer, easily the best hopes for the enlargement and improvement of youth work in this country lie with raising the skill and efficiency of the local youth worker, that is the adult who is in direct contact with young people in a youth organization.

A necessary distinction is between the leader—club leader, or Boys' Brigade captain, say—and his helpers. (Though partly for convenience, and partly because it is the less organized situation, we shall use the club situation as a model in what follows.) These two roles are different and should not be confused: it is to the leader that we address ourselves with what we hope will be practical advice.

Though these leaders are an overworked tribe, yet they should make strenuous and sustained efforts to free themselves from being so absorbed by the details of the organization, that they have no time to look at the whole enterprise, think about and plan its direction and attend to important matters outside the club events. Of course, any wise leader will maintain a personal contact with as many of his members as possible: it is tragic if he becomes recognized only as an administrator, 'that man who sits in his office for most of the evening'. But there is a serious loss of efficiency though the failure of leaders constantly to be passing the whole enterprise under review. In my observation, this rises more commonly from defects in the leader than the sheer fact of having too much to do: perhaps he cannot organize his time well or he is reluctant to delegate authority to his colleagues or he is simply an individualist, and not a good team worker. In many cases that I know, a different attitude to his responsibilities, rather than less work to do, will give the leader time to reflect upon and plan the whole enterprise.

As our main hope for improvement in the Service is a better performance by the leader of the local unit, we concentrate on possible areas of his enlarging concern and influence—at present frequently unobserved and neglected.

129

1 He should look at the neighbourhood and not merely at the organization where he works since his function is not merely to run a successful organization but to make a contribution, however small, to the social education of the young people in his district. This could have various results. He may discover needs that are not being met, and which he can offer either inside or outside the club; or amenities that are being provided elsewhere and that encourage his members to use; issues to which he can call the attention of the local Youth Committee; areas of community life which he can link with the club; in a two-way traffic system, the club both giving and receiving. (Perhaps the old age pensioners are needing help and the Rotarians are looking around for an outlet for their idealistic intentions.) He should also be an assiduous reader of the local newspaper, not only to see what is said about youth and Youth Service, but the better to understand the neighbourhood.

2 He should also leave himself enough time to be a 'talent-spotter' looking about for people in the community who have something interesting to offer to the members—and know how to offer it—either on a single visit, or occasionally, or on a regular basis. There is no insuperable difficulty here. In the club in which I worked longest, we had a leading industrialist teaching chess as well as a councillor-accountant who took the swimming class, among others. They had not been invited to participate by letter nor had they responded to an announcement in the Press: they came as a result of personal interview in which the difficulties and opportunities had been carefully explained. Of course, one does genuinely appreciate the 'less distinguished and accomplished' recruits, like the invaluable motherly soul who works in the coffee bar and whose friendliness may prove healing and acceptable to the toughest youth. But it is necessary to repeat a word which could easily be interpreted as patronizing and superior. There is of course a place in Youth Service for people of limited interests and outlook and education: the work could not go on without them: but if we are to rise to our opportunities, we also need to attract workers of a different calibre.

3 But principally, the leader of the local unit should see himself as working mainly through his colleagues—helpers and management committee—and responsible for their training to the point where they are more efficient and are also gaining more satisfaction from what they are doing. At the moment, it is pathetic to see grown men and women acting as little more than policemen and women in youth

organizations: this may even be necessary in overcrowded club rooms; but with a little of the right kind of help, these people could be so much more.

The discharge of this part of the leader's duties begins with a determined effort to have regular team meetings or staff meetings as they are usually called. Of course, there are big practical difficulties: not all the helpers come on the same evening; they themselves may not appreciate the value of the team meeting. Persuasion and ingenuity can often accomplish something. One club, in the centre of a city, laid on tea for workers once a fortnight to precede the team-meeting: it may even be worth closing the club early on one or two evenings in a session to make consultation possible. Occasional Sundays may be used for the purpose or even the residential week-end.

Team meetings are vital simply because the club cannot achieve its goals if it is staffed by a group of individualists: team work is a condition of efficiency. If the meeting is properly conducted, common goals can be explored and accepted; particular problems can be talked through; success and failure can be shared, encouragement given and morale raised; all can learn simply how to work together. Not least, the leader can learn to know his colleagues, their weakness and strength, and their potential for specialized tasks. It is a weakness of most training courses for voluntary helpers that they have thought of general skills for all, rather than specialized skills for some. The man best fitted to organize the club holiday is not necessarily the person best fitted by talents and temperament, to stimulate, sustain and supply an activity like drama or music.

The leader should think of himself and his colleagues as being involved in a continual learning and training process: but he himself will probably have to be the main agent for it. Some of the training may go on in the club through formal sessions like groups for general or specific aspects, or arranged meetings between helper and leader of a supervisory nature, or problem sessions: but much of it will be through the informal contact: and some of it, for example for specialized aspects, may take place outside the club on courses arranged by the local authority. But it cannot be said too often that the leader, without being solemn or priggish, should see himself primarily as a 'trainer' and he should not forget the members of the management committee.

He is concerned with three areas of training:

1 *Personal development* Working with young people tests the character of people, their emotional maturity, their ability to think of the needs of others, their margins of strength. Most of us who have spent many nights in youth clubs, have found limitations in our own personality: we simply were not big enough people to be as useful as we might have been for the members. Though the statement will not be acceptable to everybody, it is difficult to escape the conclusion that the leader has a pastoral role to play with his colleagues, concerned to see them grow into more secure people who do not have to satisfy their own emotional needs for significance and status in the club. There are for example not a few training groups for youth workers which have proved in the end to be fellowship or healing groups in which the youth workers have been able to work out some of their own personal problems and reach higher levels of maturity, self-awareness and self-acceptance.

2 *Understanding and information* Training for youth workers should aim mainly at an increase in sensitivity, an improvement in understanding of what is happening to members as individuals, members of groups and members of wider communities. The use of casework material is better than the giving of lectures: best of all is if they can be persuaded to write down their observations of some events in the club which can then be used for discussion. Information here relates to events, announcements, new thinking and projects in youth work.

3 *Appropriate skills* Ideally, the many gifts of different workers should make up a balanced team with informal education in a range of activities, counselling, administrative and organizational abilities well represented. But long before the ideal is reached, it is possible to discover and encourage people's possibilities. Again, training within the group and training outside the group may both be appropriate. A housewife in a Northern club was found to be an excellent teacher for a cookery class; an insurance agent was discovered to have unusual talent as a discussion group leader; a hospital clerk to his surprise learned that he was a good counsellor for young people. In each case two factors were present. The discovery of talent was a surprise and training was required.

When the full history of youth work comes to be written it will contain a chapter about how many adults found themselves when they sought to serve young people.

Notes:

1   J. B. Mays, *The Young Pretenders*, Michael Joseph, 1965, p. 19.
2   R. K. Merton, *Social Theory and Social Structure*, Free Press of Glencoe, 1957.
3   E. M. Weyer, *The Eskimos*, New Haven, 1932.

Suggestions for further reading

Chapter 1

Alicia Percival, *Youth will be led*, Collins, 1951.
S. H. Eisenstadt, *From Generation to Generation*, Free Press of Glencoe, 1964.
G. Ette, *For Youth Only*, Faber & Faber, 1949.
W. M. Evans, *Young People in Society*, Blackwell, 1966, chs. 1–5.
F. P. Gibbon, *William Smith of the Boys' Brigade*, Collins, 1934.
Leslie Paul, *The Transition from School to Work*, Industrial Welfare Society, 1962.
McGeorge Eager, *Making Men*, University of London Press, 1953.
A. E. Morgan, *The Needs of Youth*, Oxford University Press, 1938.
The Youth Service in England and Wales, The Albemarle Report, H.M.S.O., Feb. 1960.

Chapter 2

J. B. Mays, *The Young Pretenders*, Michael Joseph, 1965.
P. W. Musgrave, *Society and Education in England since 1800*, Methuen, 1968.

Chapter 3

W. E. Clegg and B. Megson, *Children in Distress*, Pelican, 1968.
G. Goetschius and J. Tash, *Working with Unattached Youth*, Routledge & Kegan Paul, 1967.
E. Hoyle, *The Role of the Teacher*, Routledge & Kegan Paul, 1969.
Department of Education and Science, *Immigrants and the Youth Service*, H.M.S.O.
Joint Negotiating Committee (1961), *First report on the Joint Negotiating Committee for Youth Leaders*, Councils & Education Press.
Mary Morse, *The Unattached*, Pelican, 1965.
D. Hawes, *Young People Today*, National Council of Social Service, 1966.
Michael Schofield, *The Sexual Behaviour of Young People*, Longmans, 1965.
D. J. West, *The Young Offender*, Duckworth, 1967.

Chapter 4

What are we trying to do?
Albemarle Report, ch. 3, 'Justification and Aims of Youth Service'.

B. Davies and A. Gibson, *The Social Education of the Adolescent*, University of London Press, 1967 (see in particular ch. 2, 'A Historical Perspective').
A. Percival, *Youth will be led*, op. cit.

Limited appeal for girls

Girls in Two Cities, National Association of Youth Clubs, published in 1967, the result of an enquiry in Bristol and Sheffield into the leisure-time needs of girls.
Mary Robinson, *Girls in the Nineteen Sixties*, N.A.Y.C., published in 1963. In addition to a discussion of the main issues contains practical suggestions and a long list of useful organizations ready to help.
Girls' Interests, N.A.Y.C., a new edition of a standard work. Contains list of practical suggestions for courses and activities and useful address list.
Jalna Hanmer, *Girls at Leisure*, available from the London Union of Youth Clubs and the London Y.W.C.A. An attempt in the London area to discover why shy girls do not use Youth Service and thus to provide teaching material for youth workers in mixed clubs. 1964.

More than buildings and organizations

J. S. Coleman, *The Adolescent Society*, Free Press, 1961.
R. Gosling, *Lady Albemarle's Boys*, Fabian Society, 1961.
Gulbenkian Foundation, *Community Work and Social Change*, Longmans, 1968.
A. Jackson and D. Marsden, *Education and the Working Class*, Pelican, 1966.
J. Klein, *Human Behaviour and Personal Relations*, N.A.Y.C., 1963.

Insulation without isolation

M. Craft, *Linking Home and School*, Longmans, 1968.
R. Keeble, *A Life full of Meaning*, Pergamon, 1965.
F. Musgrove, *Youth and the Social Order*, Routledge & Kegan Paul, 1964.
Newsom Report, *Half our Future*, H.M.S.O., 1963.
The Needs of New Communities, H.M.S.O., 1967.
Youth in Contemporary Society, U.N.E.S.C.O. Paper, 1968.

Raising workers' skills

T. R. Batten, *Training for Community Development*, Oxford University Press, 1962.
T. R. Batten, *Non-directive approaches in Community work*, Oxford University Press, 1967.
J. Macalister Brew, *Informal Education*, Faber, 1946.
J. E. Matthews, *Working with Youth Groups*, London University Press, 1966.
Fred Milson, *Growing with the Job*, N.A.Y.C. pamphlet, 1968.
J. Tash, *Supervision in Youth Work*, National Council of Social Service, 1967.

The neediest not served

A. Cohen, *Delinquent Boys*, Routledge & Kegan Paul, 1956.
F. M. Thrasher, *The Gang*, University of Chicago Press, 1927.
D. J. West, *The Young Offender*, Pelican, 1967.
W. F. Whyte, *Street Corner Society*, University of Chicago Press, 1943.

New and better forms of partnership

D. Hubery, *The Emancipation of Youth*, Epworth, 1963.
A. Percival, *Youth will be led*, Collins, parts III and IV, 1951.
Youth Work in England, Publication No. 6, University of Bristol, 1954.

Informed public support

Michael Carter, *Into Work*, Pelican, 1966.
Industrial Youth Project, N.A.Y.C., 1968.

A cadre of professional workers

A. M. Carr-Saunders and P. A. Wilson, *The Professions*, Clarendon, 1964.
V. Kent and S. Pratt, *The Working-hours of full-time Youth Leaders*, September 1961, an enquiry sponsored by the Goldsmiths' Company.
J. E. Matthews, *Working with Youth Groups*, University of London Press, 1966, chs. 7 and 10.
Albemarle Report, Ch. 6.

Index